ENDORSEMENTS

for

AN INTRODUCTION TO CHRISTIAN WRITING

"Ethel Herr has successfully nurtured new writers for years. Her *Introduction to Christian Writing* is the perfect starting point for anyone who believes God may be leading them to write."
Al Janssen, *Publisher, Author of 22 books*

"When I recommend *An Introduction to Christian Writing* both at the Greater Philadelphia conference that I direct and at conferences around the nation where I teach, I tell people that it is the best how-to book on the market for Christian writers. Not only do I appreciate all that Ethel has written in the book, I appreciate her personally and her Christian witness."
Marlene Bagnull, *Writing Teacher and Conference Director*

"Easy to read! Easy to apply! It's the best on the market, bar none! I refer to my copy all the time. I've nearly worn it out. Every writer—beginner or pro—should read it every year."
Christine Tangvald, Writer, Teacher, Conference Speaker

"It truly has become a classic."
Ken Petersen, *Acquisition Editor, Tyndale House Publishers*

If you're looking for a shining light and a clear roadmap into the complex, unpredictable world of Christian publishing, you'll find both light and guidance—and much more!—in Ethel Herr's classic how-to book, *An Introduction to Christian Writing*. Providing invaluable help, clear writing, inspiration, and down-to-earth advice, this book is a must for both the aspiring and professional writer.
Carole Gift Page, *Author, Teacher, Conference Speaker*

"*An Introduction to Christian Writing* is one of the most popular and valuable books we offer our members. We no sooner put it on the book table at our annual conference than it is sold out!"
Jennifer Ferranti, *Director, Northern Virginia Christian Writers Fellowship*

"No writer's library is complete without Ethel Herr's *Introduction to Christian Writing*. It has become the classic resource for Christian writers, and in its revised edition will continue to give solid guidance the writer can depend on for years to come. A must-have resource for every beginner."
Sally E. Stuart, *Author of the* Christian Writers Market Guide

"Good teachers aren't necessarily good writers, but Ethel Herr long ago proved she was both in her writer's "bible," *An Introduction To Christian Writing*. For years it has been a best-seller at our conference, and one of only a few I hold up annually with the exhortation that all writers need a copy. Now that it's revised, it's even more valuable. Don't just sit there, reading your reject notices—get this book today!"

David R. Talbott, *Director, Mount Hermon Christian Writers Conference*

"Ethel Herr is an excellent teacher. As a result of her book, *An Introduction To Christian Writing*, I was schooled in the craft of writing. At the same time, I was deeply instructed that whatever I do, it should be for God's glory and not mine. I've spent the last decade recommending this book to any aspiring writer who has asked me 'How did you get started as a writer?'"

Robin Jones Gunn, *Speaker, Teacher and Author, including the Christy Miller and Sierra Jensen series.*

"*Introduction to Christian Writing* is the absolute essential starting place for any Christian wanting to produce publishable writing that will compete in today's marketplace."

Elaine Wright Colvin, *Director, Writers Information Network*

Within Christian writing circles, Ethel Herr is known as a loving mentor and friend to writers who desire to express the wonders of knowing God. Her book is a practical resource for those who want to get started—but don't know how or where to begin. You can begin here... Ethel will show you how!

Joy Sawyer, *Columnist,* Inklings *magazine*

"Whether you are a beginner or a professional, you can benefit from reading this book. Despite my degree in journalism from one of the top universities in America, I read Ethel Herr's book over 15 years ago and learned a wealth of information. In the early days of my Christian writing, I highlighted many of the sentences and sections. Ethel includes practical, how-to information combined with examples and exercises. I regularly refer people to this excellent resource and I'm delighted it's back in print."

Terry Whalin, *Author of more than forty-five books*

Ethel Herr's primer is a must for every writer. I've referred to it countless times to encourage, inspire, and motivate me. She hits all the bases! This is a home run for writers!

Kathy Collard Miller, *Speaker and Author of over 30 books including* God's Abundance

"I've used it as a reference book, to look things up quickly when I need to spot check things here and there. It has been helpful to many people."

Sharon Jones, *Writer and Editor*

"You want to find out how to get started as a Christian writer? You want to know how the Christian publishing industry works? *An Introduction to Christian Writing* will tell you all this and more. Written by Ethel Herr, a woman who knows the industry, this book is full of practical, accurate information for any Christian writer.

Gayle Roper, *Author, Speaker, Teacher*

"*An Introduction to Christian Writing* is an excellent resource for the beginning or the experienced writer. It thoroughly covers the different aspects of writing, and I have used it as an effective tool in both college courses and adult education classes."

Susan Titus Osborn, *Editor, Speaker, and Author*

"*An Introduction to Christian Writing* was a total surprise. This book was user friendly. I've known Ethel Herr since... 1981. I've sat in her classes...and was enthralled with her knowledge of our craft. But to have it all in a book that focuses on the Christian reasons for writing as an act of worship means I can take a refresher course in writing and be blessed over and over."

Denella Kimura, *Poet, Teacher*

"Based on the frequent references to *An Introduction to Christian Writing* at Christian writers conferences over recent years, it has clearly helped many writers develop their writing skills. If you can afford only one writing book, this is the one to get."

Les Stobbe, *Writer, Editor and Agent*

"Reading and using *An Introduction to Christian Writing* is like taking an independent study course. In addition to the easy-to-understand nuts and bolts about writing and publishing, completing the practical assignments will move writers from wanna-be's to published authors."

Lin Johnson, *Director, Write-to-Publish Conference, Editor, Advanced Christian Writer*

"This book is an excellent resource for any speaker who is ready to take their spoken messages to the printed page and needs help on getting started. *An Introduction to Christian Writing* will help them with everything they need to know!"

Marita Littauer, *President, CLASServices Inc. Speaker and Author*

"While beginning writers will find *An Introduction to Christian Writing* a fine and authoritative do-it-yourself manual, seasoned professional writers and teachers will see it as a useful and practical text. Ether Herr, a successful writer herself, offers an impressive and comprehensive guide for anyone serious about good writing and striking a blow for the Kingdom of God."

Leonard G. Goss, *Senior Acquisitions Editor, Broadman & Holman Publishers; coauthor of* The Christian Writer's Book; *coeditor of* Inside Religious Publishing.

Ethel Herr brings a delightful blend of excellence and economy to the core issues of writing as well as a detailing of the specific skills needed to produce powerful pieces. Her book is a comprehensive course for beginners and a concise resource for more experienced writers.

Patti Souder, *Director, Montrose Christian Writers Conference*

"The emphasis on writing as a ministry is particularly refreshing...I like the examples you give the reader.... The worksheets help students think and focus... Our students have benefited from using your book."

Bobbi Beard, *Composition professor, Central Bible College*

"For a dozen years our journalism class has used *An Introduction to Christian Writing,* and it continues to receive high ratings from our students. Ethel Herr's material is probably the most practical, helpful, and honest that I have read yet. From the big picture of ministry through words to the smallest details of structure, research and tools, the author presents a clear and systematic approach to writing."

Alvin Hammond, *Professor of Inter-Cultural Studies, San Jose Bible College*

"Thank you, thank you, thank you! I just received your book on Christian writing. I have hungrily skimmed through it, and there are several ideas that I feel I can adapt to the Russian situation here. I especially like some of your thoughts in the section on developing style.

Ethel, did you ever think that one day some of your thoughts would be shared among developing Christian writers in Russia?"

Doug Wicks, *The Christian & Missionary Alliance, Russia*

"I have used *An Introduction to Christian Writing* in my writing classes and students have appreciated both its practical soundness and spiritual sensitivity. I heartily recommend it as both a textbook and as a valuable resource for anyone interested in developing their skills as a Christian writer."

Jim Reapsome, *Editor at large,* Evangelical Missions Quarterly

"I read and re-read and read again your advice about writing a book over and over again before starting my book—especially the part about 'do all you can to get out of it.' That was such good advice; because, by the time I felt it was a God-thing, there was no turning back."

Launa Herrmann, *Author*

"Rereading your book and learning more things - that He will exchange his strength for yours. This book is a winner."

Ellen Bergh, *Writer, Editor*

"Your new book is dynamite!"

Bonnie Wheeler, *Writer, CA*

"Ken and I have both devoured your writing book. He thinks it's the greatest thing since the invention of the wheel. I found the help I needed to focus on current projects."
Ken and Joy Gage, *Writers, Teachers*

"I think your book *An Introduction to Christian Writing*, is an excellent one. Thank you for writing it…I took a lot of information from your book to give a talk on writing to about eighty college kids recently"
Benny Joseph, *Teacher and former magazine editor from India.*

"Your book has been a real joy, encouragement and inspiration to me. I feel 'very ordinary' and 'very busy' as wife, mother, homemaker maintaining a very open and 'much-frequented-by-many-wonderful-guests-home,' as well as teacher for my three little ones. It's been difficult for me to overcome the discouraging feeling that I never can find time to write, and that my writing will probably never amount to anything! Many things that you've passed on in your book have really encouraged me to be more faithful to my …writing."
Mary Ligon, *Cairo, Egypt*

"Whether you are an experienced or novice writer, you will be motivated, instructed, and ministered to by Herr's book. If limited time and/or finances have squelched your dreams of taking a professional writing class, or if you just want a refresher course, consider adding to your resources *An Introduction to Christian Writing..*"
Carla Williams, *Writer, Teacher*

"*An Introduction to Christian Writing* enabled me to be published twice in the same newspaper column. When I was writing a thank-you after publication of the first, I remembered 'never leave a happy editor empty-handed.' So I roughed a draft, pulled key sentences and tagged it on the end of the thank you. The editor called and said, 'Send it.'"
Patricia Allen, *Writer*

"The perspective, unlike any I've read in the area of writing instruction displays a skillful mixture of purpose and technique. I like your description of writing as organization, making order out of chaos. I applaud you for stressing the importance of mature and intelligently sound writing. The hope and encouragement I felt while reading changed my view of myself as a writer and the potential for use of my gift."
Julie West, *Writer, FL*

An Introduction to Christian Writing

Second Edition

By

Ethel Herr

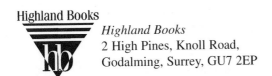

Highland Books
2 High Pines, Knoll Road,
Godalming, Surrey, GU7 2EP

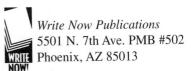

Write Now Publications
5501 N. 7th Ave. PMB #502
Phoenix, AZ 85013

An Introduction to Christian Writing - Second Edition

First published in the USA by Tyndale House 1983
This edition jointly published in the USA and the European Community
respectively by Write Now Publications, an imprint of ACW Press,
5501 N. 7th Ave., PMB 502, Phoenix, AZ 85013 (www.acwpress.com)
and Highland Books, 2 High Pines, Knoll Road, Godalming, Surrey, GU7 2EP

Cover design by Eric Walljasper
Page design by Prelude to Print

Publisher's Cataloging-in-Publication
(Provided by Quality Books, Inc.)

Herr, Ethel L.
An introduction to Christian writing /by Ethel Herr. — 2nd ed.
    p. cm.
    Includes bibliographical references and index
    ISBN 189252516X (ACW Press edition)
    ISBN 1897913508 (Highland Books edition)

    1. Christian literature-Authorship.
I. Title.

BR44.H47 2000   808'.0662
                                 QBI99-1000

Printed in the United States of America

To
Virginia Muir
who believed in this project
way back when it was just a whispered dream in my heart
and paved the way for it to become a reality.

And to
Mount Hermon Christian Writers Conference
on its thirtieth anniversary.
In this sacred spot years ago
An Introduction to Christian Writing
was conceived and nurtured into being.
Here it has continued, year after year,
to make its way into the libraries of writers
from across the country and around the world.

Acknowledgments

Books don't just happen. They grow, often slowly. From tender roots planted in well-prepared soil long ago, *An Introduction to Christian Writing* sprouted, leafed, budded, and blossomed under the watchful eyes and skillful hands of a lifetime array of literary gardeners.

I can never give credit to every gardener to whom it is due. Many names and faces have vanished from my mind. No reader would want to read the long list a better memory would produce. But a few stand out.

It will never be trite to say that my mother started it all. She aroused in me a love for books and a fascination with the writing process. She praised my childish attempts and endured my atrocious adolescent letters from college. Later, when our family lived in Europe for three years and I wrote a regular family newspaper called *The Holland Herrier,* she looked beyond its imperfections and saw a potential that only a mother could detect. "If you can ever get over being so wordy," she wrote me, "I think you stand a chance of someday becoming a recognized author."

Neither is it trite to say that without my husband this book never would have come to blossom. He helped me through my studies and encouraged me to develop my abilities. He let me attend conferences and workshops, take on speaking engagements, and teach classes, which gave me something to share and taught me how to share it.

Beyond this, I am grateful to the schoolteachers who taught me good basic skills, put up with my verbose essays, and read my awful stories. Thanks, too, to Tricia, my educator friend who gave me my first chance to teach writing skills—to her eighth-grade English students; to the adult education and private writing teachers; the writers and editors from writers conferences; the authors of writing technique books; and the members of my critique groups who guided and corrected me.

Finally, I will always thank the Lord for the women who begged me to help them answer the crucial question, "Has God called us to write?" Their confidence and faithfulness made teaching a reality, a joy, and a source of inspiration. Their success—along with the success of dozens of others who have studied this book in its first edition and who have become effective producing writers—will make the blossoms of this book increasingly bright, profuse, and robust.

Contents

Preface to the Second Edition

Back in 1983, I held my first copy of *An Introduction to Christian Writing* in my hands and read the blurb on the back cover, "Destined to become a classic text for beginning writers."

I chuckled. At least Virginia Muir, my editor at Tyndale House Publishers who had written those incredible words, believed in the book. Then I went to work giving away copies, selling copies, praying over the copies, teaching, carrying copies around the world with me. With growing wonder, I watched as God took my offering of loaves and fishes and broke and multiplied it. A host of "disciples" distributed them among vast crowds of writers hungry to learn their craft.

I know the term "classic" takes generations to be earned, but at least *An Introduction to Christian Writing* has already enjoyed a long, exciting, and fruitful life.

It has become a favorite on writers conference book tables around the country. Writing teachers use it as a textbook or a supplementary resource. Advanced writers keep it handy on their reference shelves and tell me it's well dog-eared. Several writers of note today got their start in its pages. Editors keep it on their desks and refer to it constantly, often recommending it to their writers.

It has made its way into the international market as well. One woman wrote me that she had found a copy in a tiny bookstore in a major Muslim Middle-eastern city. I put 20 copies on a book table in Seoul, Korea where nearly 4,000 Christian leaders had gathered from 180 countries of the world, and they were snapped up immediately. The leader of a woman's prayer movement in Scotland has used it to help her learn to write the story of that movement. A missionary in the former Soviet Union is using it to train Russian Christian writers. I took copies to India when I taught there. Since then, one of my students from that trip has used it to train her staff of writers creating curriculum for remote villagers. Another Indian is now writing a textbook for her own people.

Everywhere I go, the book has gone before me, making friends, helping beginners and seasoned writers, encouraging recipients of rejection letters.

When I first met Steve Laube, the editor of this edition, he said, "I feel as though I already know you. I've read your book and passed it on to so many."

But *An Introduction to Christian Writing* was written for the end of the twentieth century. As one of my reviewers in 1983 pointed out, it doesn't even mention the option of writing by computer. I read the comments and shrugged. At that time, I honestly believed that most writers, like myself, would never own a computer! E-mail and Internet and disk submissions were not even a twinkle in anybody's eye that I had heard of back then.

Today, the book continues to sell, five years after Tyndale House had to let it go out of print. It has gained the reputation of being "a classic." So, the time has come to bring it up-to-date, give it a new cover, a new publisher and send it on its way into the twenty-first century.

The original outline for this book began to take shape when I prepared to teach my first class of beginning writers. I asked myself, "If I were starting out, what are all the things I now know to be indispensable for effective writing, things I would want someone to teach me before pushing me out into the competitive marketplace?"

I jotted down ideas, sorted, rearranged, juggled, expanded, and taught these vital writing starters. Finally, I brought all my materials together and the publisher put them between the covers of a book.

In the sixteen years since then, I've taught in dozens of writers conferences and workshops, spent months researching, written reams of manuscript copy, including a trilogy of historical novels. I've also purchased and learned to use four computers and regularly communicate with e-mail and plug into the Internet.[1]

If this rewrite has posed one major challenge, it was resisting the urge to tell you all the things I've learned in the process. Several who learned their basics from this book have urged me, "Don't change it too much." Mostly I've updated the illustrations and resource list, opened a few doors into cyberspace, and tried to breathe new life into some textbookish spots.

The basic message of *An Introduction to Christian Writing* has not changed. We are God's manuscripts—eternal, unique, precious to our Creator. Each piece we write comprises, on our part, an act of worship offered to the God of the universe. From God's point of view, it functions as one more step in the process of producing His works of art in us—perfect, flawless reflectors of His image.

Ethel Herr
June 1999

---

1. I currently write on Obadiah (meaning "worshipper of Jehovah") and print out his words on Malachi ("messenger of Jehovah"). When I'm on the road it's my laptop, Ebenezer ("stone of help") and his portable printer companion, Malachi Jr.

Introduction

What Can This Book Do for You?

So you think you want to write? You may feel God nudging you toward a typewriter or computer. You may have written a few things, perhaps shared them with a friend, or even published a poem or an article. Yet, you wonder whether you should work at it hard enough to call yourself a writer. You wish someone would help you decide and show you how to get started.

Or you may be one of those self-taught writers who does it without knowing how or why. You wouldn't dare to tell the editors who have published your work that you never studied the craft. But you yearn to learn some secrets, to discover what this writing thing is all about, so you can do it like a pro.

You're not alone. Thousands of others are just like you. They're reading books, taking classes, and attending seminars and conferences on writing and publishing.

Some have unusual personal stories to tell. Lucille's conversion experience was unique. Gladys worked her way through the trauma of losing a beautiful daughter in an automobile accident. Ron and Linda were used of God in a fruitful pioneer missionary venture. Eileen was delivered by God from a homosexual lifestyle. All these people speak regularly to community and church groups. If they could write, they could expand their usefulness to a wider audience.

Some already enjoy careers in communications. Howard's pastoral ministry reaches beyond his local congregation to a thriving worldwide tape program. Margaret is a Christian school administrator who shares devotional thoughts with her teachers. Mildred has written poems, skits, and miscellaneous church program materials. Friends, parishioners, and co-workers urge these people to put their ideas into print. But they're preachers, teachers, musicians, and homemakers, not writers. Is this God's voice calling them to write?

Some write in response to an inner compulsion, but have no idea what they're doing. All his life, George has written an assortment of stories, poems, and essays. He has never shown them to anyone, but cannot seem to stop writing. Finally, he has reached a point where he must emerge from isolation and shout to the world. Gloria feels an inner compulsion to bring her idea jottings out of her daily journal and do something useful with them. Fred used to dream of becoming a writer. But the notion was impractical for a family breadwinner, so he wrote little half-completed thoughts, outlines of substantial ideas, bits and pieces, unpolished stories—and pumped gas for a living.

Some write technical things as a part of their jobs, but feel ill-prepared for publication. Nancy works in a church office, and creates weekly newsletters and bulletins. Jim is an engineer who has to write frequent reports. Can a course in basic writing techniques help them do a better job for the glory of God?

Many aspiring writers are frustrated or confused by circumstances and a lack of know-how. For years Susan worked on a book. When she finished and presented it to a publisher, she was told to go back and learn to write without being preachy. John frequently sends materials to editors and has even sold a handful of manuscripts. But he has worked entirely on his own and senses large gaps in his learning process. Judy tries to write, but four young children and a busy husband erect formidable barriers to consistency. She would give it up if she could, but something drives her back to the computer. How can these people get the training they need, learn what is normal in the life of a writer, and find some legitimate shortcuts?

In my years of writing and teaching, I have met all of these wanna-be, would-be, and already-be writers. It seems to me that they are asking one basic question: *If God has given me the gift of writing, what shall I do with it?*

Since you have singled out this book, no doubt you, too, are asking this important question. *An Introduction to Christian Writing* seeks to help you find an answer and give you the tools needed to get going.

In these pages you will find:

1. An emphasis on writing as a ministry, an avenue of personal growth, and an act of worship.

2. An exposure to the elementary building blocks of good writing. We won't assume that you already have certain writing skills. We will work on the basics of composition, motivation, and marketing—things every writer needs to know or to review in order to approach writing in a professional manner.

3. A do-it-yourself manual for learners who may not have a seasoned writer nearby to guide them.

4. A tool for teachers in search of a textbook, supplementary reading, or an outline to use either as is or in adapted form to meet the needs of beginning students.

I have divided the book into two sections—the *Textbook* and the *Appendices*. The *Textbook* consists of 11 two-part lessons, some concluding thoughts about success, several sample personal experience articles, and a resource list for writers.

Part One of each lesson deals with the writer, his person, relationships, attitudes, market study, preparation, and work habits. *Part Two* gives instruction in writing skill areas. It includes examples and assignments to help you learn. You will learn to write, not by simply reading how, but by writing. The ultimate value of this course depends upon your diligent use of these assignments.

By the time you have worked your way through the *Textbook* section and completed its assignments, you will have been introduced to all the major basic skills and theoretical motivational principles needed as a foundation for anything you will ever write. You will have written at least one manuscript (a narrative account of some personal experience), chosen a market, and learned the process of submitting it for publication.

The *Appendices* contain:

1. A glossary of writers buzz words.
   Note: When you find a word or short phrase in **bold italics** in the text, this means it is included in the glossary.
2. Helps for using this book in a writers group or class, including some suggested class exercises.
3. Additional writing exercises-outlines of other forms of nonfiction, along with assignments and checklists for critiquing them. Note: Three things you will not find here are guidelines for fiction, poetry, and drama. In the Resource List, I suggest books that can help you with these.
4. Additional information to help you as a writer, e.g., turning teaching into writing, choosing a publication option, deciding when to write a book, setting up files, starting a writers group.

If God has gifted you in the art of writing, you will find in the pages that follow all you need to get started. If writing is not your gift, you will probably make this discovery as you work your way through these same pages. Proceed prayerfully and diligently, and enjoy your journey into the life, ministry, and labor of a writer.

What Is a Christian Writer?

— The writer as a Christian
— The writer as a Worshipper
— The writer as a Prophet
— The writer as an Artist
— The writer as a Craftsman

"WRITER" was an elite title I mentally engraved on a gold plaque mounted on a shimmering crystal pedestal. I so much wanted to be one of those special people. I had taken three correspondence courses (they seemed less threatening than classes). I had even sold a few "insignificant" bits of my writing—tracts, short articles, devotionals. All the while, I read brochures about writers conferences and dreamed of one day attending one.

Then my opportunity came. Mount Hermon Christian Conference Center offered one and it was only 30 miles from home! With my husband's blessings and checkbook, I paid a ten-dollar deposit, made baby-sitting arrangements with my sister-in-law, and marched off to the fulfillment of my dreams.

Once there, I began to tremble. Standing in the registration line and rubbing shoulders with people I was sure must be real "WRITERS," I felt a dreadful urge to run. Because my husband had paid the fee and gone home with the car, I stayed. But I settled one thing from the start. At least I would not discuss my work with an editor.

However, one day at lunch I unexpectedly found myself at a table with Joe Bayly. He was not only an accomplished "WRITER" and one of the keynote speakers of the week, but he was also an important editor from the David C. Cook Publishing Company. I'll never know how it happened, but before that meal was over, I had disregarded my resolve and committed myself to a personal consultation with this awe-inspiring "WRITER," speaker, and *editor*.

Several apprehension-filled hours later, I sat in the shade of a giant redwood tree with what I decided was the kindest, most human editor alive. He put me so much at ease that I even confessed to him that I was dreaming of attempting a major project.

"I'm afraid it might be too big for me," I admitted. "How can I decide?"

In an incredibly calm and matter-of-fact manner, Joe then offered me the most valuable advice I could have received. "It's simple," he said. "Just plunge in and attack the thing as if you fully intended to finish it. If you are ready, you will know. If not, you will also know, for you will fall flat on your face."

Eager to find my answer, I went home and charged full speed into my project. Just as Joe Bayly had warned, I promptly fell flat on my face. At that point, I recalled other words of encouragement gained at that same conference, and realized that this was not the end. I picked myself up, found a simpler project, and went on. Over the next few years, I finally discovered that with no need for gold plaques, capital letters, or a crystal pedestal, I could call myself a writer.

In this book, I want to share Joe Bayly's advice with you, in my own expanded version: You'll never know whether you are gifted in writing until you attack it as if you had every intention of going all the way. Don't look back or stop to entertain the inevitable doubts. Before you finish these lessons, you will probably have a good idea where you belong. Even if you fall flat on your face with the whole writing process, you will close the book a richer person than you were when you opened it. You will learn what writing, thinking, and ministering on paper are all about. You will develop an appreciation for writers and their needs. Above all, you will become a more effective sharer of your thoughts in everyday relationship situations.

THE WRITER AS A CHRISTIAN

A writer is someone who writes. He may be a *salaried* writer who works on a payroll, performing writing functions for some company or organization. This includes editors, magazine staff writers, public relations specialists, technical writers, writing teachers.

Perhaps he is a *free-lance professional*. He writes on his own and submits his work to publishers. Not too many free-lancers make a living off their writing in the Christian marketplace. Most are part-timers who either hold down another job that puts bread on the table or have a spouse who does.

Many are *hobby* writers who write principally for the ministry or the fun of it. Occasionally they sell—more often they don't. These include authors of skits for church programs and poems for birthdays or anniversaries. Most writers do their internship at the hobby level and gradually move on to more ambitious endeavors. This doesn't mean that their "hobby" projects are any less important in the eyes of the God who gifted and nudged them to write, than the best selling novel of a famous author.

Almost everybody falls in the category of the *everyday* writer. Memos, letters, diaries—we all write something in the routine of daily living.

If you write anything at all, you are a *writer*. In these lessons, we want to help you improve the quality of your writing so that regardless of how professional you become—or do not become—you will do what you do with an expertise that is worthy of the God who has gifted you.

If a writer is a person who writes, then a *Christian writer is a writer who is a Christian*. That is, the person has a personal relationship with God through Jesus Christ. Many people who are not Christians write for Christian magazines and publishers; they address what they consider to be Christian topics. Selling to the religious market, however, does not turn just anyone into a Christian writer. Most Christian editors are deeply concerned that you, first of all, *be* a Christian if you intend to write for them. Only a Christian by experience can write from a truly Christian point of view and meet the needs of growing Christians.

Christians are members of a highly complex body of fellow-believers. Jesus Christ is our Head and gives us our typing orders. For each of us, those orders will be uniquely fitted to our individual capabilities and ministries.

Novice writers tend to look at the professionals and say, "Oh, I can't write because I can't do what C.S. Lewis has done, or Chuck Colson, or Max Lucado." How tragic! While we're excusing ourselves for not being like Luci Shaw, we're missing the opportunities to be ourselves for God on paper and to minister to the audience He has planned for us to serve. Remember, the audience you write for may never read Chuck Colson or even Billy Graham!

THE WRITER AS WORSHIPPER

Most important of all, *a Christian writer is a believer at worship*. We tend to think that we are first ministers with a pen. However, before we can minister, we must learn to worship and regard all our writing as an act of worship offered to the God of the universe. Everything we do and say must be an act of worship, done for God's pleasure. Some of our writing goes on to bless others as well, while some does no more than bless God and ourselves. Whatever else our actions and ministries accomplish, if they don't please Him, they have failed.

Worship begins in the heart of the writer. (See John 4:23,24) It is not basically an outward act performed only in public services. Worship is a personal, private act of the heart whereby I offer to God my adoration, praise, and thanks for all He is and has done for me, in me, and through me.

Worship reflects the image of God. It shows to me, and to my world through me, what God is like. In this way, as I live and write, I am allowing Him to live out His personality and His creativity in human form on earth.

Worship acts in obedience to the revealed will of God. Knowing that to present our bodies a living sacrifice to God is an "intelligent act of worship" (Romans 12:1, *PHILLIPS*) can help us decide what kinds of things to write. One woman told me she was considering writing in a genre of popular fiction that would sell well. I sensed she was not comfortable with her decision. When I questioned her, she confessed that she felt it was actually wrong and she couldn't write it with a clear conscience. God never leads us to do what will compromise, violate, or trivialize the established principles revealed in the Bible.

Worship shares openly and honestly what represents our genuine selves. During a casual conversation at my first writers conference, I heard a Professor Carl Johnson say something vital: "We must learn to write out of compression." We know the feeling—the whole world is pressing in on us and we wonder whether we can survive. We naturally want to rid our lives of all the tensions that compress us. But tensions also mold us, teach us to cope with life—and give us something to say!

A quotation has hung over my desk for years, and I refer to it often: "True creativity comes not from the removal of tension, but the acceptance of it."[1]

However, timing is vital when writing out of compression. Many writers want to start while they're still in the compression chamber. Such writing has value, but only for the writer himself. It's highly therapeutic to record your deepest inner feelings at the time of heavy compression. But these spontaneous jottings belong in your **journal**. They represent such an intense experience you may be convinced that the whole world is eager to hear all the details. In fact, they provide therapy or research, but are rarely publishable.

What the world is indeed waiting to hear is that bit of acquired insight you cannot share until you have been released from the compression chamber and reached the "hover level." (Also from Mr. Johnson.) This is the "helicopter zone"—neither too high in the clouds to allow you to stay in touch with reality, nor so low in the street that it limits your view. Here you are close enough to see the experience from an objective perspective without being crushed by the compression.

THE WRITER AS PROPHET

Once we have learned to worship on paper, we're free to think about ministering. *A Christian writer is a ministering prophet with a broken heart.* A lot of us enjoy being prophets and setting people straight. However, a study of the biblical prophets who preached judgment reveals that they never delivered many words of fire without stopping to weep and plead with God's people.

"Oh, Israel, if only you would get right with God, you could avoid all this judgment." This theme runs through the books of prophecy like a wide red ribbon. Every recorded prophetic utterance is a show-and-tell exhibit for modern prophets with a pen, revealing that rare combination of justice and compassion so typical of God. No matter how urgent the message, we must first let God break our hearts with the thing that makes Him weep, then weep with Him as we write.

Our writing as a ministry has two functions:

1. *To arrest the attention of a readership* already saturated with ideas and pressures, almost to the point of insensitivity to anything we have to offer them. Never before has it been so easy to get the printed word into people's hands. Neither has it been so difficult to get people's honest attention and to penetrate their hearts.

2. *To present all of life from the Christian viewpoint,* both to non-Christians and Christians. Our world is dying for the lack of a good, clear image of what God is like. Thousands of people have rejected some erroneous picture of God that they've seen in a church or in the lives of religious persons or in the work of non-Christians who write about things they don't understand. Few people have rejected the accurately portrayed person of God, for few have had even a fleeting glimpse of Him. In the Weymouth translation of Ephesians 1:12, Paul told a newborn church in a pagan society that they had been chosen to "be devoted to the extolling of His glorious attributes."[2] Our challenge is the same today, to provide a clear, accurate biblical picture of God.

In our prophetic ministry, God has called us to be the servants of Jesus Christ and to one another. (See Matthew 20:25-28) As servants, we will write to meet others' needs rather than our own. We will sit at eye level with our readers—admit our own weaknesses and resist the urge to preach at anyone from some imagined sacred pedestal of arrived learning.

My pastor once gave a profound warning which becomes more appropriate as outward success increases. "There is always the danger that what begins as a humble service to God will become a desire to be great."[3]

THE WRITER AS ARTIST

If the Christian as a writer is to fulfill God's best with his gift, he must also be an artist and craftsman.

When I was a child, I envied anyone who could draw and paint and produce beautiful handicrafts. Everything I tried turned to disaster. To me the message rang loud and clear—I was no artist. Many years later, I learned that art was more than painting pictures. Music is an art, as are drama, speech, and literature. Once I realized that the term *"art" applied to any kind of reflective self-expression that relied more for its motivation on beauty than utility,* I discovered that I, too, had an artistic gift from God. The artist in me enabled me to write with form, beauty, and significance. As an artist, I could bring pleasure to my reader and to God by including beauty in all I did.

I took a thoughtful look at God, who is indisputably the Source of beauty and the Master of artistic expression. I noted how important beauty was to Him. Many of His greatest treasures of natural beauty are never seen by human eyes. The intricacies of the human body, microscopic flowers, and algae tucked away in inaccessible crannies of the earth, trillions of unique snowflake patterns—God gives meticulous care to fashion each of His works with a precision and beauty we could never imitate. Then surely I don't waste my time when I polish the tiny fragments of intimate poetry in my *journal,* though I might never show them to another human being.

As an artist, I must be careful to inform my readers about man and God and His principles for functioning in this world. By producing good art, I will satisfy both my imagination and that of my readers.

> Art is ultimately organization. It is searching after order, after form. The primal artistic act was God's creation of the universe out of chaos, shaping the formless into form...[4]

Some things we write are not highly artistic literature. But because we are Christian artists, we have a responsibility, through our artistic expression, to make order out of the chaos of raw life and help our readers do the same. We can aim for at least a touch of art in everything we do.

WRITER AS CRAFTSMAN

While *art* refers to some mystical innate talent, the *craft* of writing is an exercise in the disciplines of polishing and perfecting our manuscripts. Craftsmanship is workmanship—the 95 percent perspiration that must accompany the 5 percent inspiration before a piece of art can take shape.

1. *A craftsman takes pride in his work.* He cares more about quality than salability. Remembering the worship dimension of our writing, dare we consider doing less than our best?
2. *The craftsman works with untiring diligence.* Producing simple, readable writing with profound thought content is hard work. I covet a tribute such as this one given to the Dutch art professor, Hans Rookmaaker: "He had to speak simply, because he thought so deep."[5]
3. *The craftsman nurtures growth in his person and in his writing.* He knows that easy living gives him nothing to say and when writing comes easy, he is probably not saying it well.
4. *The craftsman can take criticism and use it constructively in developing his craft.*

you teach[2], former writings, jottings in your daily **journal**, dreams and longings, strong personal interests. The most poignant ideas come from lessons learned in the struggles of daily life. Almost the entire collection of Psalms in our Bibles was written from personal pain.

> *The "heavier the cross, the heartier prayer,*
> *The bruised herbs most fragrant are.*
> *If sky and wind were always fair,*
> *The sailor would not watch the star,*
> *And David's Psalms had ne'er been sung*
> *If grief his heart had never wrung."*
> From the German[3]

2. *Your family.* Make use of familiar sayings, experiences, hobbies and skills, opinions, problems, heirlooms, bits of colorful ancestral history, and examples of solving relationship problems.
3. *Your friends.* Look at their experiences, hobbies and skills, unusual ministries, distinctive points of view, bits of insight.
4. *Your church.* Here you'll find a wide range of ideas in people, activities, programs, projects, special emphases, workable methods, sermons you hear or preach[4], attitudes.
5. *Your community.* Here is a rich source of people, industries, public services, institutions, historical events or places, organizations, social programs, landmarks, or experimental ventures of various sorts.
6. *The media (newspapers, TV, radio, magazines, Internet).* Essays, stories of people doing interesting things, or having unusual experiences, interesting but little-known facts, editorials, letters to editors, pictures, ads, classified ads (especially the personals)—all hold potential writing subjects to investigate and run with.
7. *Miscellaneous sources.* Telephone directories, books you read, conversations you overhear or take part in, letters, Bible reading, magazines in the doctor's waiting room, vacations, travel, government publications, club and association meetings, conferences, seminars, words and phrases, movies and plays, health concerns, observed problems, scientific discoveries, technological developments, current issues of social concern, interesting people you meet, gardening and home care, the contents of your purse notebook, recipes, questions that pop into your mind or that your grandchildren ask you.... The more you observe life and write about it, the longer your list of idea sources will grow.

Note: A Word About Keeping the Ideas Coming

When I began to write, I worried that I would run out of ideas. Instead I soon discovered that the process of observing my world and researching and writing each project somehow triggered more ideas.

Fearful, at first, that I might lose them, I filled a notebook with them. One day I awoke to realize that ideas were multiplying and tumbling over each other in my brain, each demanding priority. From that point on, I sent the little tormentors away, confident that the ones I really needed to hang onto would be back. Only when they returned repeatedly did I take them seriously enough to make notes and assign them a file folder. Today, I have to fight to keep ideas from sidetracking me from current projects already underway.

IS YOUR IDEA READY TO GO?

Not all ideas are ready to be shared, even when we have formed them into a coherent theme statement. Perhaps they're not complete, we're not ready to handle them adequately, or the market may not be ready for them. If your idea is going to grab an editor and keep a reader glued to the page, it must first pass the following tests:

1. *It must stay true to biblical principles and honor God.* Much current literature is tainted with the humanistic/New Age idea that we can solve all our own problems through education, right psychological approach, and/or enlightened intuition. Even Christian writers often stray from the clear teachings of Scripture into these directions. We must base our solutions on biblical teaching and write to foster a growing worship of and dependence on God.

2. *It must be interesting.* It has to matter terribly or entertain irresistibly. Are you passionate about it? If not, don't expect an editor to care. Further, does it touch the lives of prospective readers enough to excite them?

3. *It must be significant.* Significance is determined by the audience you aim for and what you intend to do for them. Are you attempting to entertain? Inspire? Inform? Whatever your goal, make your reader feel his time was well spent reading your material. He won't easily forgive you if you cheat him out of his valuable time by giving him trivia. In the words of one poet, "Poetry is found in the significance of life."[5]

4. *It must meet needs, answer (or suggest) questions, deal with problems.* Readers have physical, psychological, emotional, spiritual, intellectual, and social needs. Study people to find out what these needs are. Then be willing to admit to having needs yourself and write with the reader in mind. Make something happen, and always offer hope, which doesn't necessarily involve easy answers.

5. *It needs a universal appeal.* Is your idea so unique that no one else will care about it? Your appeal need not be universal to the whole human race, but at least to the readership you will be asking to read it. Can your target reader see himself in your story? Can he feel with you and welcome your suggestions?

6. *It must offer a **fresh new angle**.* Centuries ago, Solomon said that "there is no new thing under the sun."[6] Some subjects, or the approach to them, are spiritual **clichés**, too overworked to catch the reader's eye. Continuing to deal with a universally significant idea demands that you find some compelling new angle.

    Example: A much-written-about theme is *Bible Study*.
    > *Overworked, general approach:* How to Study Your Bible
    > *Better:* Making Time for Bible Study
    > How I Get the Bible to Talk to Me
    > Motivating Teens to Study the Bible

7. *It must still be timely by the time it reaches the readers.* Train yourself to be a keen observer who lives on the cutting edge of life. Think ahead. Allow at least one year of lead time when considering magazine ideas. A book may need five years or more. Learn to read the times and spot the trends, to anticipate what will be "hot" down the line. Occasionally God may give you an idea that seems untimely now. If it has arrested you and you can't shake it, pursue it anyway. By the time you have it ready to meet the public, it may be right in line. I've had several projects of this kind through the years.

8. *It must fit the magazine for which you want to write.* Don't send your "Tribute to Mother" to *The Christian Athlete*—unless your mother was an outstanding athlete or you slant your tribute in an athletic direction.

9. *It must be realistic.* Present an accurate, though positive, picture of life. Editors are not interested in untested theories. Admit your own failures and weaknesses, show growth and learning in your life, and the reader will be inspired to search for the same in his.

10. *Make sure this idea lies within your reach.* Begin by writing the things you know best. Later you can **research** and write about the things you don't yet know. When you consider a project that will take a great deal of **research**, make sure such **research** is realistic. If the idea proves too much for you, leave it for someone else and go on to something you can manage.

HOW CAN YOU *FOCUS* YOUR IDEA?

To **focus** an idea means to break it down in such a way that you can give the reader what he wants or needs in a form that appeals to him and in a size chunk he can assimilate.

Learn to use the **Zoom Lens Technique**—changing your writing focus from:

1. *Broad to Narrow.* Avoid expansive topics that can never be treated with any degree of significance in less than a book—or a series of articles. Break a big subject into its components, then choose one component to work with.

Example:

> *Too broad:* Witnessing
>
> *Better, but still too broad:* How to Witness
>
> *Still better:* How to Share Your Faith with a Hindu neighbor

2. *Vague to Sharp.* If your subject is too general, you will be forced to skim over the top of it and communicate nothing beyond vague generalities and ho-hummish impressions. Give your readers in-depth treatment of the specific kinds of needs they face.

Example:

> *Vague topic:* Communicating with God
>
> *Sharply focused topic:* Intercession: a Holy Partnership

3. *Distant to Close-up.* Impersonal articles, filled with high-sounding platitudes and noble biblical principles will do nothing to bring your reader close to practical shoe-leather solutions. When you open your own life and show the process of struggling and praying through to solutions based on those principles, you build a rapport with your reader and facilitate the healing of real pains and festering wounds.

Example:

> *Distant:* Trusting God Is the Key
>
> *Close-up:* Journal of a Broken Heart

SPECIFIC STEPS IN *FOCUSING AN IDEA*

1. *Decide on a general subject.*
2. *Narrow it down to a specific subject.*
3. *Ask six questions:*
   a) What do I want to say? (Theme)
   b) Why do I want to say it? (Significance)
   c) To whom do I want to say it? (Audience)
   d) Where do I want to say it? (Market)
   e) When do I want to say it? (Timing)
   f) How do I want to say it? (Structure and *fresh angle*)
4. *In one sentence summarize the single message you want to communicate.*

Note: See following sample Idea-Focusing Worksheet.

IDEA-FOCUSING WORKSHEET SAMPLE

(Working Title) **Forget-Me-Nots, In Remembrance of Him**

1. GENERAL SUBJECT: Dealing with Grief
2. SPECIFIC SUBJECT: How God can help us deal with loss of a parent to Alzheimer's
3. WHAT DO I WANT TO SAY? (THEME)
   God offers relief from the load of grief when it grows too heavy to bear.

4. WHY DO I WANT TO SAY IT? (SIGNIFICANCE)

   An increasing number of adults face mental deterioration in a parent. Many feel as I did, that, "When we lose a loved one through death, we pass through the stages of grief and go on. When we lose them to Alzheimer's, we must continue to grieve until they die." Readers need to know that God has already carried their grief.

5. TO WHOM DO I WANT TO SAY IT? (AUDIENCE)

   Any who are grieving. Even some unbelievers may find help here.

6. WHERE DO I WANT TO SAY IT? (MARKET)

   General Christian magazines (e.g. *Moody*), Take-home papers (e.g., *Power for Living*), Denominational magazines (e.g, *Pentecostal Evangel*), Senior citizen magazines (e.g., *Mature Years*), Women's magazines (e.g., *Virtue*)

7. WHEN DO I WANT TO SAY IT? (TIMING)

   Now. (If this were a seasonal article, I would plan to send it to my first targeted editor nine to twelve months ahead of the appropriate season.)

8. HOW DO I WANT TO SAY IT? (STRUCTURE AND **FRESH ANGLE**)

   2,000-word article that tells my story and includes brief 3-point summary of what the experience taught me about dealing with emotional heavies.

ASSIGNMENTS

1. Make a list of at least three ideas you might like to write about. These should be taken from experiences and knowledge you already have.

2. Using the following Idea Evaluation Worksheet for each of your ideas, decide which ones are valid. Choose one that you can write in 1,000 words or less.

3. Using the Idea-Focusing Worksheet, focus your chosen idea.

---

1. From page 6 of *Chosen Families of the Bible* by Ethel L. Herr (Chicago IL: Moody Press, 1981).

2. If you are a teacher, speaker, preacher, see Appendix Six for suggestions about "Writing What We Teach or Speak".

3. From *The Treasury of David* by C.H. Spurgeon. (McLean Vader: Macdonald Publishing Company, n.d.), Volume 2, book 1, p. 195.

4. Same as #1.

5. Elizabeth Stanton Hardy, *Poetry: the Shaping of Words* (New York: Bookman Associates, 1956), p. 22.

6. Ecclesiastes 1:9 (KJV).

IDEA EVALUATION WORKSHEET

1. Does it honor God and encourage reliance on Him? Is it true to scriptural principles?
2. Am I excited about it? Is it sufficiently interesting and significant to keep the reader glued and free from the distraction of more attractive articles on the next pages?
3. Does it meet needs, answer questions, deal with problems, or provide tools for dealing with issues?
4. Does it have a universal appeal, at least to my target audience?
5. Does it offer a fresh new angle?
6. Is it timely? Will it still be timely by the time it reaches the readers?
7. Does it fit the publication I am aiming for?
8. Is it realistic? Believable?
9. Is it within my reach? Do I know where to go to find material I will need? If you have answered "no" to any of these questions, your idea may be too weak in its present form. Consider some alterations and run the revised idea through the evaluation tests. You may find you need to put it on the back burner and let it simmer awhile longer. Don't stop, though—try another one for now. You can always come back later.

IDEA-FOCUSING WORKSHEET —————————————

(Working Title)

1. GENERAL SUBJECT:

2. SPECIFIC SUBJECT:

3. WHAT DO I WANT TO SAY? (THEME)

4. WHY DO I WANT TO SAY IT? (SIGNIFICANCE)

5. TO WHOM DO I WANT TO SAY IT? (AUDIENCE)

6. WHERE DO I WANT TO SAY IT? (MARKET)

7. WHEN DO I WANT TO SAY IT? (TIMING)

8. HOW DO I WANT TO SAY IT? (STRUCTURE AND FRESH ANGLE)

How Do I Plan My Work Area and Equipment?

"*I*f only I had an office, then I could begin to write in earnest."

Every time I hear this excuse for not writing, I recall a series of mental images collected over the years of my associations with writers and professing writers. I picture a roomy, well-equipped office filled with just the right equipment and overflowing with books and magazines. It was a writer's dream room! But for several years its occupant used it precious little, while she battled with a persistent priority problem.

I remember, too, my own big old dining room table. I picture it in at least four different houses, cluttered with papers and books and a decrepit manual typewriter. I had to clean up the mess every time I prepared a meal for my family. Before my husband returned from work, I stashed away all the evidence of my labors so I could greet him with an orderly house at day's end. On this table and under these circumstances, all my articles and poems of several years were born. My first book was written at this table.

A work area neither makes nor destroys a writer. If you want to write badly enough, lack of a proper work area will never stop you. You'll scribble notes on bits of wrinkled paper, in plain notebooks or on church bulletin covers, at kitchen counters, in the back seat of taxicabs, as you stand in line at the bank, while lying propped up in bed in the middle of the night or following a severe illness….In short, *if you are a writer, you will write!*

However, one of the greatest aids to a consistent, disciplined program of productive writing is a regular place reserved just for your special activity. Whether you can manage a spacious room, one side of the bedroom, an isolated attic cubicle, or a tiny corner of the family rumpus room, set aside for yourself a dedicated spot and hang at least a mental shingle over it that says: WRITER AT WORK.

Where you set up shop depends on you and your circumstances. Most people envision the ideal as some quaint, remote seaside cottage or a dusty attic with a songbird perched on a tree branch just outside a single grimy window that overlooks a lush garden. These may or may not be ideal, but they are generally out of our reach. Further, idyllic settings can play tricks on a fertile mind and keep us from concentrating on the thing we go there to do.

Survey your situation, assessing your family needs as well as your own. Pick the place that best suits your needs and circumstances. Set up your equipment and leave it there, if at all possible. If not, find a neat way to store file boxes, reference books, and writing supplies for easy recall during office hours. Ask for your family's understanding indulgence, but never push them out of shape in a foolhardy attempt to put your writing absolutely first, at their expense. You may join a host of other writers who find they simply have to write when the family is gone to work, school, or bed.

Once you have found a comfortable, well-lighted area, what equipment do you need in order to begin?

Pencil, typewriter, or computer? Technically, all you need is a pencil, a pencil sharpener (a paring knife will still do the trick!), and some sheets of scratch paper. If this is all you can collect, then do it! But get started! *Waiting for a top-of-the-line computer could spell the death knell to your writing aspirations and visions.*

My own journey from longhand to computer was not a welcome one. I have an inherent dislike for machines. I only tolerate them for what they can do for me. If I suspect they may turn temperamental and malfunction, I drag my feet like a notorious procrastinator. However, when I studied my first course in writing, I learned that the professional way to write was on the typewriter—even for the roughest of rough drafts.

I couldn't imagine anything as mechanical as a typewriter producing anything as creative as a manuscript. But the pros did it and so must I. I dragged out the old manual typewriter, from my college days, and made myself do it. To my great astonishment, it worked wonders.

I could now write without getting writer's cramp, and at a speed that almost kept up with the furious flow of thoughts and images that often spurted through my creative brain. Of course, I now had other problems. My fingers moved faster than the keys. In their haste, fingers were always getting out of order and producing a horrendous crop of typos, which introduced me to erasers and correction fluid.

Today, my computer has sent my fingers to flying faster than ever. I have forever retired those piles of secondhand carbon paper from my husband's work, along with the nasty bottles of thick liquid and flaky tapes that used to mess up my typewriter keys and serve as perpetual roadblocks.

Like it or not, we live in an electronic age. The old days of submitting only paper manuscripts are gone and I can send a 400-page book manuscript via e-mail in less than ten minutes! So, whether we write longhand, type, or use a computer, we are all forced—either on our own or by hiring another's services—to reproduce computer disks or e-mail manuscripts, if we aspire to publication.

Perhaps there will always be some writers who feel a freer flow of creative juices when they grab a pen or pencil and push it across a yellow scratch pad the way Jessamyn West did it, or C.S. Lewis. I confess, I still often begin a piece this way. But once the thoughts begin to flow, I rush to my now beloved computer and let them gush.

Paper and printers. For rough drafting, you won't need any special kind of paper. Make sure your sheets are uniform in size and that you write on one side only. Discarded sheets of paper still clean on one side make excellent rough draft stock. My husband brings me stacks of such paper from his work. Other good sources include copy stores, stationers, schoolteachers, junk mail letters... Look around you. One more use for your sharpened observation skills.

For the manuscript you submit to an editor, be choosy. Buy good white bond paper—preferably 20-pound weight. NEVER use shiny copy papers, indistinct or pale dot matrix printed sheets, or handwritten pages. (See Lesson Eleven, Part One for detailed instructions on preparing a manuscript for submission.)

File boxes. High grade steel filing cabinets are a valuable long-term investment. In the beginning you may need to settle for something a bit less expensive and space-consuming. For years I used a couple of cardboard file boxes. Corrugated paper boxes from a copy shop work well. You'll also need folders, dividers, card files, and cards. Or you may choose to file data on your computer. *Just be sure you keep a backup system updated, with at least three removable disks of each manuscript or category of items.* If you've ever watched a neighbor's house go up in smoke in 15 minutes, or plugged in what was yesterday a perfectly valid floppy disk and discovered the data was all gone, you'll know the importance of faithfully creating those pesky multiple backups! I always make sure my husband has an updated disk copy of my important manuscripts in his desk at work at all times.

Envelopes. For mailing manuscripts, photos, and illustrations, you need sturdy manila envelopes. Ideally, they should be in two sizes—9x12 and 11x14. For enclosing a *SASE* (see Lesson Eleven, Part One for explanation), you can put the smaller envelope inside the larger. If you have only one size envelope, you can fold your *SASE* in half.

Desk and chair. If you can't have a real desk, any sort of table will do as long as it's the right height so you can sit comfortably without hunching over your work. It helps if the table is large enough to accommodate the stack of books and papers you are working with. A separate typewriter or computer table helps as well.

Writers grow quite ingenious when creating makeshift tables from things like ironing boards and doors mounted on two-drawer filing cabinets. My husband built my first desk from old moving crates. It served as a marvelous transition from the dining room table to the secondhand desk I later purchased with my earnings.

Make sure the chair you use fits your body, allows you to plant your feet on the floor, and is firm enough to keep you alert. An investment in a good chair can save you a lot of chiropractor bills!

Miscellaneous supplies. Keep a ready stock of supplies such as pencils, pens, erasers, paper clips, cellophane tape, scissors, staples, ruler, glue, postage scale, and stamps.

Finally, you will need a writer's reference library. You can begin small and add to it gradually. I suggest you begin with a dictionary, a synonym finder, a manuscript preparation guidebook, grammar and usage books, a marketing guidebook, and some basic Bible reference books. In addition, you can use a variety of specialized books to help with your specific genre of writing. (See "Resources for Writers") For the area of expertise that provides you with ideas on which to write, keep a special shelf for *research* and resource books, e.g., parenting, Christian education, devotional books.

If God has called you to write, no matter how unpromising your circumstances may appear, you can make them work. As long as you wait for the ideal place and equipment, you'll never write a word. Find the best place available, gather whatever tools you can and go to work without any further delay.

Writing the Personal Experience Story

- Why begin with the personal experience story?
- What is a personal experience story?
- Using the personal experience story
- Techniques for writing the personal experience story
- Steps in writing the personal experience story

If Mary of Nazareth were living today, imagine how many editors, TV, and radio show hosts would be clamoring at her door for story materials. I can hear it now.

"What were your secrets of mothering, Mary?"

"What was it like to raise a perfect child?"

"How did you deal with friends and neighbors who didn't believe He was Who you said He was?"

"Can we sign a contract with you for the exclusive right to issue your full-length biography? Think how many people you can help."

No woman ever had a more fantastic story to tell. Yet, almost all God has given us are her words to the angel and her prayer known as the *Magnificat*. We read that she wondered and pondered the things that came her way. Beyond this, the Scriptures give us only a couple of vague and passing glimpses of her point of view.

From Mary we learn that not all stories are meant to be told. From the writers of the Gospels (Matthew, Mark, Luke, and John), we learn that many are. In fact, until you have learned to tell a story on paper, you are not ready to write much of anything else either.

WHY BEGIN WITH THE PERSONAL EXPERIENCE?

1. People love to read about people—doing things, feeling things, struggling, suffering, achieving, winning, growing. One of the oldest cries from human lips is "Tell me a story!" A story increases readability, because it builds bridges between author, reader, and idea. The apostle Paul had stories in mind when he wrote: "My message and my preaching were not in persuasive words of wisdom, but in demonstration of the Spirit and of power, that your faith should not rest on the wisdom of men, but on the power of God." (1 Corinthians 2:4-5 NASB)

2. As you attempt to zoom in from distant to close-up writing, nothing works better than an experience from your own life. It comes from where you live, breathe, and care.

3. To write a story from your life teaches you to think through an event and discover its significance. You take the raw facts of your life, organize them, decide on a theme, and offer something of value for your reader's life.

4. Learning to write a story gives you a foundation for all future writing ventures. Before we are ready to write abstract truth, we need to learn to tell a story to illustrate that truth. Look at God's writing methods. In the Scriptures, He gave us *personal experience* stories to illustrate every truth He communicated. Most notably, He gave us the vivid pictures of His Son. "The meaning of the Incarnation of Jesus Christ is the message that God is the God of struggle, that He knows complexity rather than shortcuts, that whatever else is true in the universe, it is true that God is united with hurting, suffering, struggling humanity."[1]

WHAT IS A PERSONAL EXPERIENCE STORY?

A *personal experience* story is an account of some real-life happening told in such a way as to convey meaning to life. There are two kinds of *personal experience* stories:

1. Dramatic happenings, with a universal appeal.
2. Common happenings told dramatically, again with universal appeal.
   In both cases, we must take care to show that the real drama happens on the inside of our characters, where truth communicates meaning and fosters growth.

USING THE PERSONAL EXPERIENCE STORY

You will use your story in one of these three ways:

1. As a full-length *article* (1500 words or more) or book. It will recount a complex story with plot that develops progressively toward a climax. Such stories demonstrate character growth, usually as the result of a protracted struggle. (See "Forget-Me-Nots")

2. As a short, concise story centered around a single incident with one simple and obvious point for the reader to carry away. Known as **fillers** (tiny bits of materials that fill in spaces on a magazine page), these run in length from one short paragraph to a thousand or 1200 words.

3. As an **anecdote**, a "short account of some interesting or humorous incident."[2] **Anecdotes** either introduce or conclude an **article** or book (or chapter of a book), or they appear sandwiched in between other kinds of writing in an **article** or book. (See "Intercession: A Holy Partnership", under "Sample Articles") They serve the following purposes:
   a) Illustrate a point
   b) Liven up an article
   c) Change the pace of an article—allow the reader to breathe
   d) Introduce the subject arrestingly
   e) Inject a touch of humor
   f) Make a point memorable

TECHNIQUES FOR WRITING THE PERSONAL EXPERIENCE STORY

1. *Make it special.* No matter how exciting and extraordinary the story, if you approach it in a dull, reporting fashion or if you draw from it some timeworn hackneyed application, it will be too common to gain a respectful hearing. Learn to use your story's unique **slant** and emphasis so that it shows character development. This makes a profound impact on your reader.

2. *Be succinct.* Aim for both brevity and clarity. This demands a delicate balance between two potentially contradictory needs:
   a) *Conciseness.* Express yourself in as few words as possible, stripping the narrative of unnecessary elaborateness and beside-the-point rabbit trails.
   b) *Thoroughness.* Take whatever time and space you need to tell the story well, give it color and emotional impact, and be sure it conveys the intended message believably.

3. *Be honest.* Resist the temptation to pad the facts and/or gloss over or omit shady areas. Don't set yourself up as the perfect example of truth in action. Begin your story at a point where you're facing a problem, making a blunder, or becoming aware of a personal weakness. Let the reader watch you grow and change as God, family and friends help you learn to cope with the problem, forsake your foolishness, or overcome your weakness. Remember that your reader cannot identify with, or take advice from, a know-it-all who has "arrived."

4. *Be positive.* You are a dispenser of hope to a desperate, negative world. If you can't offer at least a hint of a solution, then don't bother to share your problems or frustrations.

5. *Don't preach or moralize.* Avoid such statements as "Now as you can learn from my experience…" Present your story without giving the impression that your experience is the only normal one for all people in similar circumstances. God does not deal with us all in the same manner. Besides, you are writing an illustration of truth, not preaching a sermonette.

6. *Show—don't tell.* Roll out all the multi-media equipment and make sensory recordings of colorful sights, sounds, smells, textures, moods, tensions. Use active verbs, clear picture nouns, keen mood perceptions. Transport your reader on location and ensnare him in your story as it happened and as you felt it.

7. *Write both to the head and the heart.* Let your complex person come through the words on paper. A simple logical presentation of facts is newspaper journalism at its basic minimum. This is not your goal in writing the **personal experience** story. You aim, rather, to involve the total person of your reader in order to interpret and give meaning to someone else's life through your story.

8. *Make it sound convincing.* Truth is often incredible when presented in its raw form. Remember that one of the functions of art is to create order out of the chaos of real life. An important part of this process is writing a believable story. Identify the factors that make the story real and introduce them; e.g., the power of God and/or the indomitability of a determined will make many otherwise incredible stories believable.

9. *Include strong* **reader takeaway.** Never leave the reader with the question "So what?" If your story is indeed trivial and has nothing to offer, file it under "Practice Pieces" or "Performance Rehearsals" and go on to something that can help the reader, not simply presume on his time.
   Note: Occasionally the only takeaway value your story has is to make the reader laugh. (See Lesson Eight, page 144 for more about the validity of humor.)

10. *Structure the personal experience as follows:*
    a) **Problem** (Admit to having one.)
    b) **Solution**—or decision that there is none (Show how you struggled to come to this conclusion.)
    c) **Outcome** (Show results of applying solution or coping with inability to find one.) Let reader see what you learned and how you grew.

11. *Emphasize the theme of your story by choosing one of the following three methods:*
    a) **Straight** *narrative.* Tell the story and let it stand alone, making sure the **theme** is inherent in the story. (See "Forget-Me-Nots")
    b) **Narration** *plus a summary*: Tell the story, then add a commentary or a summary of points. (See "Slow Down and Live")
    c) **Framed** *narration*: Set your story in a beginning-and-ending *frame.*

This introduces a concept, then tells the story as an illustration either with or without a short application at the end. (See "Intercession: A Holy Partnership")

STEPS IN WRITING THE PERSONAL EXPERIENCE STORY

1. *Find a quiet place.* Spend an hour there writing down all the details you can remember about the experience you decide to write. Don't worry about order or accuracy of chronology or facts. Just jot down things as you recall them. Concentrate on sensory data (colors, textures, sounds, smells, bodily sensations), moods, reactions, personalities of people you interact with, Scriptures, dialogue, lessons learned or problems suggested.... Record every memory of the event, down to the most trivial detail.

2. *Read through what you have written.* Ask yourself these questions and others they may trigger:
    - Do I need to **research** anything? Street names? Dates? Reasons for the event? Other things going on in our country or the world at that moment?
    - What facts need to be checked? In library? Old newspapers? By telephone? By letter? By computer? Do I have old letters or **journals** that will help me clarify the story?
    - Whom do I need to talk with? Family? Friends? Children of deceased people involved in the story? Someone who can help me with doctrinal or scriptural problems? (For more help with **research**, see Lesson Seven, Part Two.)

3. *Fill out the Project Plan Sheet below.* You will be working from this as you go on.

4. *Organize and plan your story.* (See Lesson Eight, Part Two)

5. *Write your story.* (See Lessons Nine and Ten, Part Two)

6. *Rewrite and polish your story.* (See Lesson Eleven, Part Two)

7. *Submit your story to a publisher.* (See Lesson Eleven)

ASSIGNMENTS

1. Prepare a specific place for your working area. Begin to assemble equipment and plan for what is yet needed.

2. Take the personal experience story idea you have chosen and follow Step 1 of the procedure in this lesson.

3. Study two personal experience stories in the "Sample Articles" ("Forget-Me-Nots," "Slow Down and Live"). Analyze each story to see how it used the special techniques listed in this lesson.

1. Jerry Harvill, "The Real Questions of today's Seekers," from *Discipleship Journal,* Issue 37, p. 37.
2. *American Heritage Dictionary of the English Language, 1973.*

PROJECT PLAN SHEET ————————————————————————

General Subject:

Specific Subject:

Working Title:

Theme (What one thing do I want to say through this story?):

Purpose (How do I hope my readers will respond to this story?):

Form for using Personal Experience:
  Full-length article?
  Short filler?
  Anecdote as illustration in a larger work?

Approximate Length:

Target Audience:
  Age
  Education
  Occupation
  Interests/Needs

Possible Publications: (You'll find help with this in Lesson Seven, Part One)
Items needing research or verification:

STRUCTURAL ANALYSIS WORKSHEET ─────────────

UNITY

1. What is the theme of this piece?
2. What is the point of view?
3. What tense does it employ?
4. What mood does it create?

Are all these things consistent throughout the piece?

COHERENCE

1. Circle all transitions. You may want to draw arrows to show what things they connect.
2. Indicate logical development. Mark events in number sequence (e.g., 1, 2, 3,... or 5, 1, 2, 3, 4, 5). (See Lesson Nine for more explanation.)

EMPHASIS

1. Mark each technical tool used with an E, followed by the number on the list of ten emphasis tools on pages 137-138, e.g., E9 for Plot because Plot is number 9 on the list.
2. Mark all false tools (wordiness, improper mechanical techniques, preachiness) with an X. (See pages 136-137) You may ask yourself which proper tools could have been used in their places.

PART 2

Organizing the Story

- Slant your material
- Choose a literary form
- Outline your story

You have a story to tell. Through the first seven lessons of this book, you've been getting ready to tell it. You have a file folder filled with facts and ideas, quotations and memories, research questions and market possibilities, maybe even some pictures and newspaper clippings.

What next? How do you turn this precious raw material into a sharp little story that your chosen editor will snap up in a hurry? In this lesson, we will look at the three steps to organizing your material so you can begin to write.

STEP ONE: *SLANT* YOUR MATERIAL

A slant is an approach to a story that makes it meaningful to a specific reader. Read through your jottings and your **Idea-Focusing Worksheet** from Lesson Five. Look for a key or a *theme* that will draw the facts together and give you a *slant*.

There are two methods of slanting. One is the *shotgun* method, in which you tell the story with no thought for how best to arrest the attention of your reader. You spread your ammunition in a general direction, hoping it will hit a target, somehow, somewhere. The second method is the *pistol* method in which you aim carefully at a specific spot and deliver your *theme*-oriented story with precision. Obviously the second method is the only one worth your efforts.

Pistol slanting takes some careful planning.

1. *Know your material.* Do you still have some vital questions unanswered? Go after them. If they prove to be unattainable, then you must either
   a) scrap the project
   b) shelve it until a later time when you may find the answers
   c) find some other angle by which you can avoid missing materials and still have a valid story.

   Does your story present problems of interpretation? Often the process of analyzing the story will give you the resolutions. If this fails, then let the story lie until you can deal with it.

2. *Know your **theme**.* What one thing are you trying to tell your readers? State it in a single simple sentence. Themes usually fall into one of the following categories. Study these examples:
   - *Question theme:*
     Do family holiday celebrations have any spiritual value?
   - *Set-of-facts theme:*
     My child needs to know ten things before he starts school.
   - *Adventure theme:*
     God protected us in a civil war riot in a Third World country.
   - *Problem theme:*
     How I learned to survive the morning rush to get my family out of the house.
   - *Place theme:*
     A visit to a tiny church in Spain taught me to value my freedom of worship.
   - *Inspirational/moral theme:*
     How a vacation taught me to relax and apply the therapy of God's handiwork to jangled nerves.
   - *Biographical vignette theme:*
     What I learned about the peace of God from watching a friend die of cancer.
   - *Personal opinion theme:*
     Why I believe in strict home discipline.
   - *Doctrinal theme:*
     A surprising experience taught me the meaning of God's justice.

3. *Know your purpose.* What are you trying to do for your reader? All writing is done for one or more of these four reasons:
   - *To entertain*: engage reader's attention, make reading enjoyable, interests, amuse, please, tantalize, excite. As Robert Frost once said of a poem, it "begins in delight and ends in wisdom."[1]
   - *To inform*: educate, share facts and opinions, reveal
   - *To stimulate*: arouse the reader to think or feel something, either in agreement or disagreement with you.

– *To persuade:* change the reader's mind and arouses to action

Most of the things we write, as Christians, are for the purpose of **persuasion**. We know that when it comes to spiritual truth, we can't rely on our cleverness alone. It is ultimately the work of the Holy Spirit to affect true spiritual change.

However, God has given us the tools of creative communication and He expects us to be wise in our use of them. As we plan and write our pieces, we need to know how communication happens, based on this diagram.

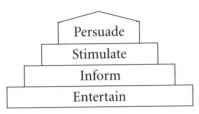

Four Basic Purposes of Writing

These four purposes build on one another (See diagram). In order to inform a reader, you must first get his attention (usually by entertaining him at some level). You cannot stimulate him to think or to feel without informing him. Certainly you cannot persuade a reader without stimulating him.

4. *Know your market.* Here is where all that time-consuming market analysis pays off. It tells you how to **slant** your material and aim with pistol precision to reach your target audience.

STEP TWO: CHOOSE A LITERARY FORM

In Lesson One, we noted that when God wanted to say "I love you" to the people He had created, He did it partly through *word choices*. He also did it through the *wide variety of literary forms* He employed.

He has given us hundreds of *stories of recorded history*. Many show His compassionate *providences;* e.g., creation, an ark for a devastating flood, plagues and a cloud by day and pillar of fire by night. Others give us delightful *surprises,* e.g., a rainbow of promise, manna on the ground, a talking donkey. There are *love stories* that illustrate His love, e.g., Ruth and Boaz, the Bride and Bridegroom in the Song of Solomon, Hosea and Gomer.

Even His *laws* reveal something about His love; e.g, Ten Commandments, Proverbs, and rules for building the Tabernacle and Temple.

He speaks lavishly of His love in the inexhaustible store of *poetry* in the Psalms, Ecclesiastes, Song of Solomon, and Lamentations. Prophets employ *drama and mime.*

Jesus uses *fiction* in His parables and common items of daily life in dozens of *object lessons*, e.g., Vine and branches, loaves of bread, lilies of the field.

The Book of Revelation is built on *dreams, visions,* and *messages* delivered by angels.

Begin today to study His many varied forms. (See Appendix Three, "God the Master Wordsmith") Soon you will find yourself looking for them in every Bible study you do for the rest of your life. You, too, can study writing technique from the Master!

1. *Learn about the forms from which you can choose.* They are almost limitless. Here are a few:
    - *A Prayer:* Opens your heart to God on paper so the reader learns by listening in.
    - *A Poem:* Gives the germ of an experience and some observation made or lesson learned from the experience. Usually short and limited to one sharp emotional idea phrased with imagery.
    - *A **Narrative**:* Tells a story chronologically, either with or without interpretive comments called "*frames.*"
    - *A Journalized Story:* Tells a story, using dates, as if it were recorded in a journal. Usually includes intense personal reaction to events.
    - *An **Article**:* Presents a **theme**, usually with a set of points, and illustrates them with **quotes, anecdotes**, statistics, supporting data. The **personal experience** story will serve either as an introduction, a **frame**, or an illustration of a point.
    - *An Open Letter:* Tells a story as if in a letter to a friend, organization, or public person. This form allows you to inject a great deal of personal reaction and interpretation.
    - *Fiction:* If based on **personal experiences**, it changes names, places, even circumstances. It may end up being quite unlike the real experience that inspired it.
    - *Essay:* Takes a personal story and makes it the basis for an expression of opinion about some matter of vital importance to the reader.
    - *Nostalgic Humor:* Recounts some past event or lesson learned, emphasizing the value of reflection on the past as encouragement for the present and the future. What about clean, decent humor for the sake of humor? It makes us laugh at ourselves and see the lighter side of a ponderous life. It shows us the logic of some important lesson. Tickling the funny bone can touch the reader where he might never let serious material even come close.
    - *Travelogue:* Tells the story of some trip you took. A difficult form to master. Like a "home movie," unless done extremely well, it will

bore everyone but the author. Successful travelogues have unusually significant and interesting angles and adhere tightly to their *themes*.

- — *Vignette or character sketch:* Tells a story of another person as seen through your eyes, showing admirable qualities or important lessons you learned from your subject.
- — *How-to*: Shares the step-by-step process by which you accomplished some feat or solved some problem of importance to a reader.
- — *Exposé*: Points up a problem of a universal nature and suggests some realistic way to work toward its solution. Note: As Christians, we have a responsibility to dispense hope, not despair. An exposé for the purpose of telling the world how bad something is must be balanced with some sort of hope for a cure. Otherwise, we give the impression that God has absconded His throne and left us stranded.
- — *Full-length book:* Gives the depth your story may demand. Don't attempt this as your first project. Pick a smaller story and practice your craft before you launch into a book.

2. *Study examples of the different forms.* Which ones are most effective? Why? Would you feel comfortable working with them? Do they fit your story?

3. *Experiment with several forms.* Don't write off any form as impossible for you before you have given it several honest tries. You'll never know what you can do until you experiment.

STEP THREE: OUTLINE YOUR STORY

1. *Why outline?*
   a) It helps you develop your ideas in logical sequence.
   b) It helps you achieve unity, coherence, and emphasis, because it allows you to see an overview of your piece before you write it.
   c) It helps you to spot and correct many structural difficulties, such as roaming among the buttercups.
   d) It helps to provide continuing momentum for the writing process. A completed outline guides you from one point to another and prevents many mental blocks between points.

2. *Kinds of outlines.*
   a) *Point Outline* (used mostly for articles)
      Consists of:
      1) Introduction
      2) Body of the article (points)
      3) Conclusion

    b) *Chronological outline.* Lists events in sequence as they happened (e.g., 1,2,3,4…)

    c) *Chronological-in-a-frame outline.* A **frame** is a point of contact which makes the telling of your story meaningful to the reader:

       Opening frames may consist of:
- A theme statement
- A question related to the **theme**
- One event in your story lifted out of sequence to get attention, because it points directly to your story problem.
- A startling statement related to the **theme.**

       Closing frames may consist of:
- A theme statement
- A summary
- Application questions or challenges.

3. *Making an outline.*

    a) Collect your materials—sheets of paper or index file cards. Bring together in one place.

    b) Sort your materials
      1) Read through your notes.
      2) Jot down different points, idea categories, or events in sequence.
      3) Search for possibilities for an attention-getting opening that will give a clue to your **theme.** (See Lesson Nine, Part Two)
      4) Put your points in order. Shuffle them around, if need be until they fit together logically. Eliminate unnecessary points and ideas, and save them for use in another story. Limit to three points.

    c) Make a simple skeleton outline with notations of sources, **quotes**, and **anecdotes** you plan to use to fill out the piece. An alternative is to make an outline complete with all your subpoints, perhaps even written in sentence form. I personally have difficulty with this kind of outline, but it may help you.

    d) Some accomplished authors do most of the outlining in their heads. *Don't try this while you are learning the steps.* One basic rule in writing is this: You can break almost every rule once you learn to write, but first you have to learn to live by them so you will know when and how to break them.

SAMPLE SLANT WORKSHEET

(For article, "Slow Down and Live")

1. *Subject:* Time and energy management.
2. *Theme:* If you want to survive emotionally, you have to learn to slow down and enjoy living.
3. *Purpose:* To inspire readers to take life at a livable pace.

4. *Target audience*: Busy people (especially wives and mothers).
5. *Market ideas:* Denominational, women's, family, single parenting magazines, adult take-home papers.
6. *Form*: Narrative with concluding frame of five summary points and theme.
7. *Point of view:* First-person intimate (I-You).
8. *Tense*: Past for narrative. Present for application.
9. *Mood*: Serious, inspirational, motivational.
10. *Length*: About 1,000 words.

SAMPLE OUTLINE WORKSHEET

(For article, "Slow Down and Live")

1. *Subject*: Time and energy management.
2. *Working title:* Slow Down and Live
3. *Theme statement*: "Be still and know that I am God…They that wait upon the Lord shall exchange their strength for His."
4. *Surprise element*: How God answered my panicky prayer and changed a paradigm.
5. *Outline type*: Chronological-in-a-frame.
6. *Lead (Opening)*: Standing in front of a mirror, praying for an ulcer.
7. *Bridge (Transition phrase)*: "The trouble had begun a year earlier."
8. *Development of Body:*
   a) Beautiful dreams
   b) Dreams turned into nightmares—work load increased
   c) Crisis point—panicky prayer
   d) Resolution—God's answer and healing
9. *Conclusion (Summary frame):*
   a) Five lessons to be shared with overworked readers
   b) Present attitude toward work and rest
   c) Theme statement (Scripture quotations)

ASSIGNMENTS

1. Analyze "Slow Down and Live" using the **Structural Analysis Worksheet** (Lesson Eight, Part One).
2. Study the slant of this same story, using the **Sample Slant Worksheet** and **Sample Outline Sheet** above.
3. Create an outline for your own personal experience story. Fill out both the **Slant Worksheet** and **Outline Worksheet** below.

1. Frost, Robert, "The Figure a Poem Makes" in *Writers on Writing,* ed. Walter Allen (Boston MA: The Writer, 1948), p. 22.

5. Ethel Herr, "Forget-Me-Nots," p. 9.
6. Ethel Herr, *The Dove and the Rose,* p. 96.
7. Ethel Herr, "Forget-Me-Nots."
8. Ethel Herr, "Slow Down and Live."
9. Ethel Herr, "Intercession: A Holy Partnership."
10. Ethel Herr, LMPF prayer letter, November 1989.
11. Ethel Herr, "I Took Off My Badge," *The Young Calvinist,* March 1970, p. 5.
12. Ethel Herr, LMPF prayer letter, April 1997.
13. Ethel Herr, "What Matters Most" from *Moody,* May 1992, Moody Bible Institute. p. 25.
14. Lee Wyndham, *Writing for Children and Teen-agers* (Cincinnati: Writer's Digest Books, 1968), p. 125.

PLAN WORKSHEET

Working Title:

Forget-Me-Nots, In Remembrance of Him

1. Theme sentence:
   a) God offers relief from the load of grief when it grows too heavy to bear.
2. Lead:
   a) Finding a package of forget-me-not seeds in an appeal for funds for Alzheimer's research and how it mocked my grief.
3. Transition:
   a) "The bright, capable woman I remembered was gone."
4. Body (Middle):
   a) Mother's failing health and memory
   b) My failure to handle the changes
   c) A Scripture verse that began the healing
   d) Progression of dealing with the problem over the following months
5. Ending:
   a) Another package of forget-me-not seeds tested my new freedom from grief.
6. Twist (Surprise element):
   a) I'm ready to plant the seeds, in remembrance of Mother and Him.
7. Special effects tools:
   Forget-me-not seeds
   Timing of the reading of Isaiah 53:4

What Do I Do with My Completed Manuscript?

— Idea to Publication

Congratulations! You have achieved something many aspiring writers never see. You have come to the end of your **rough draft**. Did you pen across the bottom of the page in calligraphic script, the distinguished message: "FINIS"? What now?

Put it in a drawer and forget about it.

Forget my brainchild? you think. *When the world needs it so desperately NOW?*

Or perhaps your reaction is the opposite. You feel like my student, Barbara, when she handed in her first completed story. She held it firmly in outstretched hands and explained, "I want you to know I'm smarter than this."

Regardless of how you feel about your work at the end of your **rough draft**, it is neither ready for the editorial desk nor the wastebasket. It needs to cool off. You can't possibly begin to see it objectively for at least another week. (Remember the *Creative Cycle,* page 87)

The journey from inspiration to publication is a long one. Few of the steps can be rushed, for at least two reasons:

1. Writing is an art and must grow at its own pace.
2. You are dealing with busy editors in a competitive marketplace.

At this point, it helps to chart the route from idea to printed page and take a good look at the steps we have not yet dealt with in our studies.

IDEA TO PUBLICATION

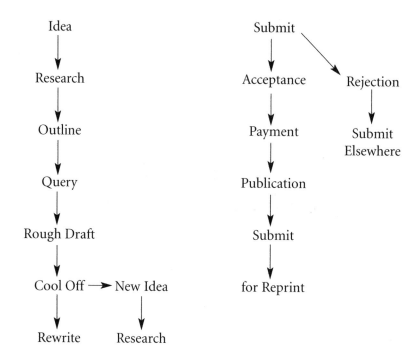

Idea → Research → Outline → Query → Rough Draft → Cool Off → New Idea

Cool Off → Rewrite

New Idea → Research

Submit → Acceptance → Payment → Publication → Submit for Reprint

Submit → Rejection → Submit Elsewhere

THE QUERY

In a *query* letter, you explain your article or story idea, showing its value to the reader and your ability to handle it convincingly. You solicit the editor's interest.

Once you've written a number of pieces and have an accurate feel for your capabilities, you will write a *query* letter to an editor before writing the story. While you're still learning to compose a piece, write it first, then send a *query*.

Do not send queries for short fiction, poetry, or *fillers*, unless guidelines from your target publication indicate it is required for all materials. A few editors indicate in their guidelines that they prefer to see only completed manuscripts.

Do send a query whenever the editor requires it. Query before writing the article or story if: (1) each magazine on your possibility list would demand a different treatment or slant, (2) the piece will involve a lot of research and/or expense which you would not pursue for any other reason, or (3) your idea is so specialized that only one market would be interested in it.

Query letters predispose an editor to read your manuscripts with interest. They keep the door open for your manuscript in case someone else queries about a similar piece. They may save you many hours of wasted **research** and/or writing of an unsalable piece. The editor's reply to a query should help you in slanting and organizing the material to suit the market.

Note: Some things you will want to write regardless of whether they will ever be published or not. Publication is not the only or even necessarily the highest goal for every piece you ever write. More about this in the CONCLUSION.

TYPES OF QUERY LETTERS

1. *The idea query.* Present a synopsis of the idea or story and perhaps include a couple of **anecdotes,** quotes, and/or facts of special interest.
2. *The outline query.* Present the idea and enclose an outline. Outline queries are particularly helpful if you are writing an article or treating some subject which has several angle possibilities.

COMPONENTS OF THE QUERY LETTER

1. *Subject.* Be as specific as you can. e.g., Not "Prayer," but "Intercession: A Holy Partnership".
2. *Specific thesis.* In a single sentence, what you are trying to say to your reader.
3. *Working Title.*
4. *Style.* Try to pinpoint your approach: anecdotal, personal experience, straight reporting, humorous, etc.
5. *Your credentials.* What authority and ability do you have to write this piece? Include writing **credits**, if you have any. Otherwise, give qualifications such as firsthand, teaching or research experiences you have had in the particular topic area. Never say, "I'm a beginner, so I have no credits." Then make your query so professional the editor will never guess your secret.
6. *Reader benefits.* Will it inspire, inform, encourage, give tools for coping…?
7. *Questions for the editor.* These deal with how you should treat the piece—slant, word length, and the like.
8. *Photos.* If you have photos to send, indicate this and explain what type they are, e.g., b/w, transparencies, digital, etc.
9. *Time Frame.* If possible, give some realistic idea of how soon you plan to have the completed manuscript ready for submission.

GUIDELINES FOR WRITING EFFECTIVE QUERIES

1. *Be prepared.* Do sufficient **research** so you know where you are going. Preferably write a tentative lead before you query. Including an attractive lead can go a long ways to selling the idea.

2. *Be brief.* Preferably make it no longer than one page of single-spaced printing, almost never more than two pages, plus an outline.

3. *Be professional.* Address the editor by name. (Obtain name either from guidebook, guidelines, or by telephoning the publisher and requesting it.) Print your letter neatly (No faint or fuzzy dot matrix, slick paper, or smudged typing with strikeovers or erasures.). Single-space, except between paragraphs. ALWAYS include a **SASE** (self-addressed, stamped envelope). Make sure you have all details correct (spelling of names, dates, sources, facts). Submit only one idea at a time. Also, study the market guides and editorial guidelines before submitting a query, so you are sure you have chosen the correct market.

4. *Be reader-conscious.* Don't simply tell the editor why you are excited about the piece, but rather why the readers of your target magazine will be eager to read it.

5. *Be at your best.* The **query** is your sales pitch, your only opportunity to make a good first impression on the editor. Write and rewrite with care, but don't overdo the effort so as to destroy naturalness. Make the query a lively sample of your best writing. Let your enthusiasm for the subject and your concern for excellence shine through this letter.

FOLLOWING UP THE QUERY RESPONSE

1. If the editor answers your **query** with a "sorry, we are not interested," pick the next market on your possibility list and submit a new query.

2. If the editor responds with suggestions for changes in your outline or approach, get ready to oblige the request as much as possible. Think of the editor as a member of your communication team, not an obstacle you must lop off en route to publication.

3. If the editor says, "Send us your article on speculation," **this is not a promise to buy it**. It is simply an invitation to send your finished article for consideration. "**On speculation**" or "on spec" are the buzz words.

4. With this kind of go-ahead, the ball is in your court. Carry through on all promises you have made. If the editor gives you a deadline, meet it. When this is impossible, work out a reasonable alternative with the editor. *Never ignore a deadline.* The basic principle here is to *give editors every reason to be more than glad they decided to look twice at you and your manuscript!* You want your name always to bring a smile to their lips, not a groan to their hearts or a pain to their heads.

ROUGH DRAFT

This is a danger zone. Watch for the following snares:

1. *Premature writing.* You may experience a tendency to rush into the writing before you've done adequate **research**. Some **research** was necessary before

you wrote your *query*. More may be needed now. Do your homework and resist the temptation to produce a flawed or substance-thin manuscript.

2. *Wordiness paranoia.* Some writers, in an effort to avoid too many later revisions, write skimpily in **rough draft**. They leave out facts and impressions that are vital to an understanding of the story. With practice, you'll learn to control the size of the **rough draft** without sacrificing essential information. For now, within reason, don't worry about word limits. Get it all down and cut in later drafts.

COOL-OFF

During this excruciating period, you lay your precious work in the drawer and restrain yourself from retrieving it to examine it every five minutes. In the heat of excitement over your work being accepted **on speculation**, resist the temptation to omit this crucial step. Now is the time to turn your mind to new ideas and research projects. You may develop some valuable **spin-offs** from your first project—ideas that were suggested by your research but didn't survive the sorting-out process of outlining.

I wrote "Slow Down and Live" to share the important learning that had come to me through a painful experience with overcommitment. As I worked on it, I realized I was not covering all the bases. My deep feelings of frustration toward some people who were pushing me in directions I couldn't go finally surfaced in a poem, "Please Let Me Be Me." Later two more poems on the same topic emerged. These were **spin-off** projects that represented new learning and perspectives I had gained as I grew through the experience.

REWRITE

Your week is up and you release that magical pile of papers from its dark prison. Now with renewed vision and objectivity, you begin cutting, rearranging, picking, and polishing. We will look at this process in detail in Part Two of this lesson. A good critique group can help you at this point (see Appendix Ten). Remember, your manuscript may have to pass through several more cooling and rewriting periods before it reaches the point of polished professional finesse that qualifies it for the journey to an editor's desk.

SUBMIT

1. *Prepare the manuscript neatly.* Type or print out on a computer or word processor double-spaced, on one side only of good quality 20-pound 8-1/2" x 11" white bond paper.

   Note: NEVER USE CORRASABLE BOND PAPER, COLORED PAPER, SHINY PAPER, OR POOR QUALITY DOT MATRIX PRINT! Make it as easy for the editor to read as possible!

Leave a margin of one inch on each side of the page. (See **Sample Manuscript Typing Guide** below). Keep a copy of your manuscript for your files. Also prepare and fill in a **Submission Record Form** (see sample form, following the typing guide). Attach this record to your manuscript copy and place it in your work folder along with accumulated outlines, research notes, working drafts, and correspondence related to this project.

Prepare and add appropriate information to your **Market Record Form** (see sample below). Save this form either as a computer file, in a notebook, or on cards in a card file. This enables you to keep track of which manuscripts you have sent to each editor.

2. *Send the manuscript in one or more of three ways.* Be sure to find out which method(s) your editor prefers. Electronic methods are truly remarkable—a far cry from the old type-and-hope-for-no-errors-and-make-carbons method that I had to use for my learning years. Some editors may even require that you provide them with at least a disk. Others will still ask for a hard copy in addition to any electronic copy you send them.

   a) *Printed manuscripts* of two or three pages may be folded like a letter and mailed in a regular legal-sized envelope. Longer manuscripts should be sent flat in a large manila envelope. Always enclose a *SASE* (Self-Addressed Stamped Envelope—may be folded) for the editor to use when returning the manuscript.

   b) *Disk manuscripts* fit nicely into a cardboard mailer which you can purchase at your office supplier. Enclose return address label and postage. Mark the disk well with manuscript title, file name, type of machine on which it was made, operating system (e.g., Windows 95), format (e.g., Text Only), and the word processing program (e.g., Word 6.0) you used.

   c) *E-mail documents* attachments can also transport entire manuscripts. Check with the editor before using this method.

3. *Send to only one market at a time,* unless you have marked it **"Simultaneous Submission"** in the upper right-hand corner. Generally send only one manuscript to a market at one submission. One exception is poetry. You may send three to five short poems at one time.

   In the upper right-hand corner, you will indicate one of the following designations, indicating which *rights* you are offering to the publisher:

   a) *First Rights Only:* Editor buys the right to print your material for the first time only. After it is published, rights revert to you and you can resubmit the material elsewhere. *This is the most common designation you will use.*

   b) *Reprint Rights:* Editor buys the right to reprint published work, but only after it has been released by the first publisher.

MANUSCRIPT TYPING GUIDE ———————————

NAME ————————————   About 1,000 words   A

ADDRESS ————————————   Rights Submitted

CITY STATE ZIP ————————————   B

SOCIAL SECURITY NUMBER ————————

TELEPHONE, FAX, E-MAIL ————————

                                                     1

                                                     2

                                                     3

                                                     4

                                                     5

                                                     6

                                                     7

                                                     8

                                                     9

                    TITLE.. 10

                    BY.. 11

                    NAME.. 12

                                                     13

                                                     14

                                                     15

FIRST LINE OF TEXT   16

    Numbers on the right-hand side represent double-spaced lines   17
down the page. Title, "by" and Name are to be centered on the page. If   18
you type on a computer, use this page as a model for preparing your   19
page. If you use a typewriter, actually create a sheet of paper like this   20
and put it behind your blank sheet in the typewriter, with numbers pro-   21
truding beyond the sheet, to the right, so you can use them as a guide.   22
Succeeding pages begin with your name in the left-hand corner, on line   23
A. The text will begin on line B.   24

SUBMISSION RECORD FORM ──────────────

Title _____ **Words** _____

Submitted to:	Date Sent	Date Sold	Payment	Date Returned	Postage

Gross Proceeds _____
Net Profit _____

MARKET RECORD FORM

(File this information in computer file, on 8 _ x11 notebook paper, or on a file card)

Periodical Name _____
Address _____
Telephone _____ **Fax** _____
E-mail _____ **Website** _____
Editor _____
Publisher/Organization _____

Ms. Title	Date Sent	Sold	Date Returned	Date Purchased	Rights	Payment

    c) *Second Rights:* Editor buys the right to print materials for the second time. Better to offer reprint rights.

    d) *All rights:* Editor buys the sole rights to publish writer's material in whatever form he desires. No editor can purchase these rights without a signed permission from the author. Sometimes when you endorse a check from the publisher, you are accepting the assignment of all rights. Some editors will reassign rights upon request, after first publication. *Don't offer all rights unless the editor refuses to buy any other kind.*

    e) *Book Rights Reserved.* This is technically covered by the "First Rights Only" designation, but many writers will also add these words, "Book Rights Reserved," just to ensure that there is never a question. You may have no idea now that what you write will end up in a book someday. But remember that little acorns into giant oaks do grow!

4. *Affix sufficient first-class postage to both the outer envelope and the* **SASE.** Book manuscripts may be sent via UPS. In this case send money for return shipping in a separate letter. Don't use fourth-class book rate. It's allowable for manuscripts, but is slow and not given priority treatment by the post office. *Show your editor that you feel your work is worth the best of care.*

5. *Wait patiently for an answer.* Be skeptical of all market-guide promises of prompt replies. Program your mind to anticipate a delay. Don't bug your editor, writing or calling him every few days. Such action will probably encourage him to return your manuscript so he will not be subjected to further hassling. After an unreasonable delay (three to six months), however, it is proper to write a courteous note inquiring about your manuscript.

NEXT PROJECT

Now that your first story is in the mail, your mind is free to concentrate on the next idea. As you submerge yourself here, time will pass quickly and one day you'll receive an answer from the first editor and exclaim, "Already?"

ACCEPTANCE OR REJECTION

At last the day comes—your inevitable encounter with truth. The postman brings you a sharp, businesslike, legal-sized envelope with the magazine's logo in the upper left-hand corner. Inside you find a letter of acceptance and perhaps a check (if publisher pays on acceptance). Your joy is complete. You hug the postman, your spouse, your children—and the dog.

Or the envelope you hold in your hand looks discouragingly familiar. Your **SASE** is now unfolded and postmarked, bearing the manuscript in company with a form rejection slip (or a personal letter, if you are unusually blessed). Search the contents carefully, and you just may find that although your work is being returned, the editor is asking you to rewrite and resubmit it.

Drop everything else and rework this now, returning it as soon as possible. Don't let the idea grow cold in the editor's brain. Worse yet, don't wait till the person who believes in your work has moved on to some other publishing house and a new editor comes on board with a whole new set of guidelines which your manuscript may not fit.

If your story is accepted, sit down immediately and write a thank-you note to the editor. This may constitute paragraph one of a new *query* letter concerning your current project. Of course, if the new idea is not right for this same market, send the new *query* elsewhere. Wherever possible, though, suggest another idea and follow it up. *Never let a pleased editor forget you.*

If the moment of truth was rejection, take heart. This is recycling time. Pick the next magazine on your list. Type a new query letter (if required) or send the manuscript off this very day. *Never let the sun go down on a rejected manuscript!*

Make it a practice from the beginning to ask God to guide you, at least in part, through the responses of editors. Take these Scripture verses as your motto:

> Dear brothers, is your life full of difficulties [and rejections]? Then be happy, for when the way is rough, your patience has a chance to grow. So let it grow, and don't try to squirm out of your problems. For when your patience is finally in full bloom, then you [and your manuscript] will be ready for anything, strong in character, full and complete. (James 1:2-4, TLB) (author insertions in brackets)

PUBLICATION

If you thought the acceptance day was exciting, wait for this one! When you hold in your hand your very first published manuscript and see your name in print, along with those words you labored so hard to produce and polish, the whole world turns to sunshine and a rainbow of colors.

If for the next few days you find yourself calling all your friends to invite them over for coffee and just happen to have the magazine lying open on your coffee table, or if you set it on your kitchen counter, dresser, or mirror—wherever you will see it a hundred times a day—consider yourself normal. But don't settle down to a long life of full-time celebration. You have more projects to write and they won't get done while you are giving tea parties to doting friends

Actually, this may not even be the end for your manuscript.

SUBMIT FOR REPRINT

Now begins the process of once more submitting it to other magazines—this time for reprint. You may submit them either as "***Simultaneous Submissions***" to magazines with non-overlapping readerships (mostly denominational markets) or to one magazine at a time. This time, in the upper right hand corner you offer "Reprint Rights." Always include a cover letter indicating where the piece has been previously published and when.

Your story may not be immortal—at least not quite. Yet it will live on. The words you write today may circle the globe in a suitcase, be read on the radio, find their way into a movie, video, or TV production, be chosen for inclusion in an anthology, enter a prison cell in a stack of outdated magazines—on and on it can go.

No matter how old your story grows, the time is never too late to thank God for it—for what it did for you, for the editors who liked it and gave it a distinguished birthing, for each reader whose life has been touched—or ever will be touched.

Rewriting and Polishing
the Final Version

- In defense of rewriting
- The mechanics of rewriting
- Objective of rewriting
- Four-Reading Method for rewriting
  and polishing

*T*o tell the world you are a *WRITER*
May make you think you're smart.
To complete a fifteenth rewrite—
Believe me, that's an art!

Your **rough draft** has lain tucked away in a drawer for at least a week. Meanwhile you've been filling your mind with new ideas, market studies, **query** letters, maybe even some **research** or writing exercises. At last the time has come to rouse your sleeping brainchild and groom him for his long trip to the editor's conference room.

This lesson will lead you through the exacting and sometimes painful process we call Rewriting!

IN DEFENSE OF REWRITING

Nothing you write is chiseled in granite. No matter how inspired you felt when you wrote your manuscript or how good you thought it was when you wrote *Finis* across the page, it is not sacred, inspired, infallible, and possibly not even terribly good. Lest you grow discouraged with the need to rewrite, remember this. Even the pros don't write—they rewrite or re-re-rewrite. One of the signs that a pro is a pro is that he is willing to cut and rewrite as many times as it takes to make his work come out just right.

Rewriting helps to ensure that:

1. We have said what we intended to say.
2. We have made our work believable and understandable.
3. We have made it interesting, smooth, captivating, and significant to our target audience.
4. We have made it marketable.

THE MECHANICS OF REWRITING

What method is best for rewriting? This depends on the writer. Experiment and find the methods that work best for you. Certain things are essential for all rewriting:

1. Write copiously and fully in the **rough-draft** state. Leave plenty of room for cutting.
2. Type the **rough draft** double or triple space, leaving generous margins for ease in penciling in corrections. Even if you do all your rewriting on the computer, use double-spacing for ease in reading as you go.
3. Don't start revising too soon. Don't shortcut the cooling-off periods.

Other specific approaches differ with the writer and his subject. Here are a few of the standard ones:

- *Blue pencil:* This terminology goes back to the early newspaper days, when all writing was done on a manual typewriter without correction fluid or tape, and changes were literally made with a blue lead pencil. Even though I write on a computer, and don't even own a blue lead pencil, I still print out what I've written and begin with a red pen or an erasable pencil. Here, I mark things out; encircle words and phrases; draw arrows; and scribble in revisions, corrections, additions. This method can get messy and hard to read after a time. As a variation on this old theme, I often use sticky notes where I can experiment with whole new sentences or paragraphs and discard the ones that don't work.
- *Cut and paste.* When I did the first edition of this book, I literally cut and pasted bits and pieces of the manuscripts to rearrange them. I tired of the semi-permanency of glue and discovered staples. (The memory makes me shudder!) Today, I do the nasty job with a few quick clicks and dragging operations with my nifty little computer mouse, but the function is still referred to as "Cut and Paste."
- *Fresh start.* This one works well when the mess gets illegible. I even use it on the computer as well, starting over with a new screen and a fresh version of the old story. At times, the momentum gained

by retyping facilitates the thinking process. This book, for instance, was first written on a typewriter. So, when I brought it out for revision, I had to enter the entire book in my computer. At first I groaned, then discovered something marvelously creative happening as I touched each word with my fingers, giving it a *fresh start* approach.

No matter how many fresh start files I compose, I still keep copies—either hard or computerized—of every version. I may change something, then decide later to go back to the original. Or often passages that I have cut from an earlier version fit beautifully into some other slot later on.

— *Critique group*. This method is generally reserved for the time when you have done all you know to do with your manuscript on your own. Then you take it to your group for objective help.

OBJECTIVE OF REWRITING

Regardless of the mechanical method you use, your objective is the same:
1. To cut superfluous words, sentences, and paragraphs.
2. To add new words, phrases, and ideas.
3. To rearrange words, sentences, paragraphs, and ideas.
4. To reword for increased smoothness and effectiveness.
5. To correct errors of grammar, spelling, punctuation, and word accuracy.

Warning: Two subtle dangers can easily sabotage your rewriting process. Be aware of them both.
1. *Not enough revising and cutting.* Extraneous words, poorly arranged sentences or phrases, tedious repetitions, inaccuracies, general sloppy constructions.
2. *Too much revising and cutting.* My children once had a book with a poem about a woman who had a maniacal penchant for scrubbing. She scrubbed everything ceaselessly. One day she scrubbed her children's faces so much they disappeared. I think of this every time I've reworked a manuscript until I can no longer see it objectively. That's when I especially value my critique group to help me decide how close I am to obliterating my brainchild's face.

FOUR-READING METHOD FOR REWRITING AND POLISHING

The basis for this method is a series of four complete read-throughs of your manuscript. It helps you learn to search for the four different kinds of things that you need to check in polishing your work. Eventually looking for these things will come naturally to you and you may not need to do separate read-throughs. For now, follow them meticulously.

FIRST READING:

CHECKING FOR **INTENT**: THE **COMMUNICATION** DIMENSION

Read your manuscript ALOUD straight through, stopping only to make notes and marks in the margins for reworking later. As you read, ask these questions:

1. What is my *thesis*? Can I state it in a sentence?
2. Did I say what I intended to say? (The critique group or an impartial reader can help you with this one.)
3. Is my idea significant? Stimulating? Timely? Practical?
4. Did I narrow my *focus* sufficiently so that I could develop my *thesis* adequately? Or did I try to cover too much territory and end up not saying anything well?
5. What is unique or fresh about my *slant* on the subject?
6. Did I make this manuscript appealing to my target audience? Is my style appropriate (language, mood, depth level)? Are my illustrations geared to the right age, doctrinal, or interest group? Do I have the right authority image to reach this audience?
7. Does the form I have chosen for this piece enhance its effectiveness in reaching my target audience? If not, should I change the form? Or should I consider a different audience?
8. Did I meet the editorial requirements of my target publication? Word length? Type of materials? Subject matter? *Style* of writing? Special requirements (taboos, lead types, doctrinal stand)?

SECOND READING:

CHECKING FOR **CONTENT**: THE **ARTISTIC** DIMENSION

Read the entire manuscript ALOUD again—this time making some changes as you go. Ask yourself these questions:

1. Are all my statements perfectly clear?
2. Are they honest expressions of my beliefs or of the beliefs of those I have quoted?
3. Are there inaccuracies or things I need to check for accuracy (facts, quotations, sources, names, etc.)? Are my ideas and facts adequately documented?
4. Do I offer hope to my reader? Am I fair in my presentation of the issues? Do I ignore sides of an issue that I prefer not to deal with?
5. Have I used colorful word pictures to communicate abstract concepts? Is my dialogue realistic?
6. Have I avoided preachiness? Dullness? Triteness?
7. Is my *viewpoint* realistic? Are my points practical or are they too theoretical or technical to be of any value?

8. Have I controlled my writing so everything is related to my *thesis*? Are there whole paragraphs or sections of buttercups I need to omit?
9. Do I have an arresting beginning? A logically progressing middle? A punch-packing, memorable ending?
10. Are my *transitions* clear and effective?
11. Does it read smoothly? Does it drag? Is anything awkward or out of place? Are my ideas in the right order?
12. Have I placed emphasis in the proper places? Have I used short, poignant statements? An element of surprise?

THIRD READING:
CHECKING FOR **DETAILS**: THE **TECHNICAL** DIMENSION

Read the manuscript ALOUD for the third time, picking at it for all those nasty little details that can make the difference between slovenly and masterful work.

1. Is my *style* simple or cluttered? Sincere or affected? Appropriate to my subject?
2. Are my paragraphs properly divided? One thought per paragraph? Plenty of white space on the pages?
3. Are my sentences varied in length? In the right order? All necessary? Written in complete thoughts?
4. Have I overused any words? Have I used unnecessary words?
5. Have I chosen colorful words? Action words? Specific words? Accurate words? Appropriate words? Simple words? Precise, correct words?
6. Have I used clichés?
7. Have I committed errors of grammar? Have I switched pronouns? Switched tenses? Do I have shoddily constructed sentences? Uneven parallels? Run-on sentences? Disagreement of subject and verb?
8. Have I committed errors of spelling? Punctuation? Capitalization?
9. Have I relied on dashes, exclamation marks, italics, and quotation marks to do what proper word choices and arrangement should accomplish?

FOURTH READING:
CHECKING FOR **RESPONSE**: THE **IMPACT** DIMENSION

Give your manuscript to an impartial critic to read. Ask that person these questions:

1. Did it interest you? Mildly? Intensely? Unusually?
2. Did it make you feel anything? What?
3. Did it stimulate you to think? To reconsider your ideas?
4. Did it arouse you to do anything? To change any attitudes?
5. Did it strengthen the convictions you already held?

As you work over your manuscript and use all these questions, you may sometimes be tempted to toss the whole idea out as a bad dream. DON'T! Stop first and do four things:

1. Review your gifts as a writer. Ask God to help you evaluate them from His point of view.
2. Recognize where you are in the Creative Cycle.
3. Recall the rewards of becoming a writer. Read this promise God gave to Jeremiah:
    > "If you return, then I will restore you—
    > Before Me you will stand;
    > And if you extract the precious from the worthless,
    > You will become My spokesman." (Jeremiah 15:19 NASB)
4. Renew your commitment to
    > "run with patience the race…looking unto Jesus the author and finisher of our faith." (Hebrews 12:2-3 KJV)

ASSIGNMENTS

1. Write a query letter for your personal experience story to the editor of your first choice of market. This is a practice letter. Don't send it until you have completed polishing your story.
2. Polish your personal experience story. Share it with your critique group if you have one. Finish polishing your piece. When it is ready, prepare it according to the format in the lesson; then submit and go on to another project. See Appendix Four for more writing exercises.
3. If you are ready to form a critique group, study the guidelines given in Appendix Ten.

Should I Write a Book?

"You mean you've had a book published?"

How often I am asked this by some overawed stranger who has just learned of my profession. The words always weigh heavy with wonder and incredulity—a reaction not far removed from worship. Our society has the idea that to publish a book is to "arrive," to become an unusual human specimen.

To write and publish a book *demands a tremendous amount of disciplined thinking, heart-searching, and dedication to duty*. When done right, a book results from excruciating effort.

Further, *it involves a special kind of process, quite different from the production of a shorter work*. It demands a unique level of stick-to-itiveness to live with the same project for months, even years, without tiring of it or losing powers of intense struggle.

I never recommend a book project as a starting point for beginners. Yet, because so many would-be writers approach the writing discipline with a book idea in mind, I want to give you some suggestions and checklists to enable you to determine whether indeed you are ready to think about writing that book that seems to be calling you. In order to sort out the romance from the reality of your dreams and fit them into a practical time frame, you need to answer three basic questions:

1. Is my idea a *book* or an *article*?
2. Should *I* write this book? If so, am I *ready* to begin?
3. How shall I *prepare* to write this book?

IS MY IDEA A BOOK OR AN ARTICLE?

A book *is not*:

1. An article on a simple subject, padded with enough anecdotes, descriptions, philosophizing, quotations, and the like to fill 100 or more pages.
2. A loose collection of vaguely related articles, vignettes, poems, sermons, or other short works.
3. A detailed autobiography or lengthy family history that fascinated the writer and therefore is as sure to sell as popcorn at a football game.

A book *is:*

1. A work of 10,000 to 100,000 words or more.
2. A work with complexity of idea and strength of theme adequate to sustain a reader's interest for the period of time it takes to dig through all those thousands of words. (It may be an anthology, or collection of articles, poems, stories, even sermons. However, these need to be so tightly unified in theme and form that the reader is unaware that they are collections. He thinks of them, rather, as a complete book unit.)
3. A work that usually demands a great deal more research than an article. You need many more quotes, statistics, illustrations, opinions, and bits of local color for a book than for an article. All of these are necessary, however, not for padding, but as a part of developing a significant theme.
4. A work with sufficient interest intensity to arrest the reader all on its own and convince him it's worth the price he must pay. A magazine article will go home with the reader who buys the magazine out of loyalty to the magazine (often by subscription), for the pictures, or for some other articles, feature materials, or authors found in that same issue. A book has to draw the reader on its own merit and deliver what the cover promises.

To distinguish an *article* from a *book* idea, ask yourself:

Is my idea sufficiently complex, practical, colorful and intensely interesting to entice thousands of readers to part with their money to buy it, then give it the hours required to carry them through its several thousands of words and be glad they read it?

SHOULD *I* WRITE THIS BOOK?

The chances are that provided your idea is truly significant, timely, and needed, if you don't write the book, someone else will. In fact, the idea has probably occurred to some editorial committee, and they may be looking for the right person to write it. When they see your proposal, they will immediately ask, "Is this the right person and the right manuscript for this idea?"

If you are convinced the answer is "yes," you must be prepared to defend that conclusion before you approach the editor. To determine these answers, do a lot of praying as you go through the following checklist.

Until you have answered all these questions with complete honesty, you're not ready to consider writing a book!

SELF-APPRAISAL CHECKLIST

BASIC CONSIDERATIONS: DO I KNOW WHAT I'M TRYING TO DO?

1. Why do I want to write this book? To acquire fame or fortune? To spout off anger or expose some evil that makes me panicky? To minister to the needs of the Body of Christ? To fulfill my dreams? To prove myself to someone?
2. Who is my target audience? Age group? Occupational group? Sex? Interest group? (Visualize your reader sitting across the room from you as you write.)
3. What do I want to say? Can I summarize my theme in a twenty-five to fifty-word paragraph? (If not, your idea is not clear enough to work on or even test for validity.)
4. What response do I expect from my readers? Mental or spiritual stimulation? Change of mind or attitudes? Worship? Action? (Be specific.)

RESPONSIBILITY: DO I DARE TO WRITE THIS BOOK?

1. Am I convinced enough of my ideas that I dare to put them out into nationwide (or international) circulation where they will affect thousands of lives? (If not, wait until you've wrestled with your concepts long enough to be sure.)
2. Does my priority-and-duty system allow me to expend the time and energy required to finish this book? (It will demand far more time than you can imagine now.)
3. Will anyone be hurt by this book if I write it (family, friends, organization, Body of Christ, name of Christ)? Using a pen name is not always an adequate safeguard.

VALIDITY: IS MY IDEA VALID AND WORTH A COMPLETE BOOK?

1. Do I strongly believe in it myself? Will I still believe in it ten years from now?
2. Does it carry intense interest value for my target audience? For how wide an audience? (A publisher must sell at least 10,000 copies to break even on his investment.)
3. Is it helpful? To the people I want to reach? To how many people?
4. What new angle or original viewpoint do I offer? How is my approach different from similar books on the same subject? (Your approach must set it apart from the other books close to it.)
5. How urgent and current is the theme? Can I write it and get it out in time to meet the needs I'm aiming for? Is it so tied to contemporary issues that it will be outdated in a year or two? If so, is the need for it sufficiently

urgent to warrant the sacrifices (e.g., personal, family, ministry, quality of workmanship) demanded in order to produce it in time, under pressure?

6. Does it offer hope to my readers? Can I be positive in my message? Do I have problem solutions to share or am I interested only in exposing difficulties and leaving the reader numb with shock and despair? Do I know how to point the reader to God as the essential problem-solver to be consulted and trusted?

7. Is it a sensational story? Does it glorify man and/or describe sin so graphically that God's grace is not the predominant picture planted in the reader's mind? Is God clearly at the center of focus in this book idea?

8. Is there enough material available and does this idea offer sufficient depth and interest content to make it worth a whole book? Or would I do better to confine it to one or more articles?

QUALIFICATIONS: AM I THE RIGHT PERSON TO WRITE THIS BOOK?

1. Have I had sufficient experience or training in the subject area to qualify me as an expert?

2. Do my credentials give me an adequate authority image to enable the editor to sell my book? If not, can I change my slant to reflect an area where I do have authority to speak? (e.g., Lacking a history degree, I could never write a biography of William of Orange, but I could write a series of novels that portrayed much of his biography.)

3. Do I know how to do the research this project will demand? Is such a process practical for me at this time?

4. Am I genuinely excited about this project? Enough so that I can live and work with it for at least the next year or two without growing tired of it?

5. Am I willing to research the market thoroughly in order to find the best outlet for my book?

6. Do I have the patience to wait until my research is complete before I start writing? To set the project aside for a time, if need be, until I know the Lord wants me to push ahead with it? To accept long delays in the editorial and publication process as a part of God's perfect timing?

7. Can I take criticism and suggestions from editors? Am I adaptable and willing to work with editors on business details?

8. Am I prepared to take the time and effort to reply to and pray for all who will respond to this book with pleas for attention, fellowship, clarification, and help of various sorts?

Someone has said that any Christian book that will bless people's lives must first cost the writer a great deal in personal learning and growth as well as hard work. *Am I willing to make whatever sacrifices this project may involve, for the glory of God through my work?*

HOW SHALL I PREPARE TO WRITE THIS BOOK?

1. Learn to write and market articles, poems, stories, fillers. Master the disciplines of scheduling, planning, polishing, marketing, and editorial relationships with small items before tackling the gigantic challenges of a book. This is the process of *becoming a writer*. Don't launch into the book field prematurely, but plan on a long internship, remembering that God has as much time as it takes to get you ready to do His work in His way.

2. Become familiar with the following categories of books on the Christian market:

   a) **Personal experience books**: Stories of what happened to the author, how-to and self-help books about things the author has learned to do or problems you have learned to solve or cope with.

   b) **Personal expression books**: Devotional and inspirational books, opinion books, books in the Christian living category.

   c) **Research books**: Historical background, Bible studies, commentaries, resource books, histories of the Church, missions, denominations, historical biographies.

   d) **Other people's books**: Biographies, modern histories of families, organizations, missionary ventures, anthologies of essays or articles on a theme, modern translations of old classics, personal stories of other people done in one of several ways:

      1) Straight third-person narrative, with author's byline.

      2) *First person* as-told-to: e.g., Susan Smith *as told to* Mary Jones.

      3) *First person*, with author: e.g., Susan Smith *with* Mary Jones.

      4) *Ghostwritten* books in which the author writes someone else's story, and only the subject's name appears in the byline. Author's name is not mentioned in such books, even though author receives a percentage of the royalties. Many authors and editors (myself included) find this practice unethical, as it gives the false impression that the person whose story it is, is also a writer.

   e) **Co-authored books or *collaborations***: Books written by two or more people, with equal bylines: e.g., Susan Smith *and* Mary Jones.

      CAUTION: Other people's stories and ***collaborations*** are the most dangerous types of books to write and are *definitely not recommended for beginners*. The number of sticky problems (both financial and social) that can emerge from such arrangements defies the most fertile imagination. Before you even consider these types of books, establish yourself as a writer and chalk up a lot of practical experience with editors and the business end of writing. Whenever anyone asks me to collaborate with them, I always tell them that I have no time for more projects, *and* I value our friendship too much to jeopardize it with a collaboration.

3. Decide which category your idea fits, then read samples of those types of books. Study them for structure, technique, significance, style, and use of language. Ask the following questions of each book you read at this stage of research:

a) Did I enjoy it? Why or why not?

b) What was the number-one outstanding impression it made on me? What is the theme? How significant is it? Did the author stick to it or ramble off on a dozen tangents?

c) What was the author's tone? Impassioned orator on a soapbox? Prophet with a broken heart? Psalmist at worship? Teacher come alongside to guide the reader? Dull lecturer? Entertaining storyteller?

d) What makes this book unique from others on the same topic? What authority does the author have to write it? Does the author come across as having all the answers? Or as a learning, growing person still struggling with important issues?

e) What makes this book effective? Or ineffective? Would I recommend it to my target audience of readers? To some other audience? Why or why not? What are its strengths? It weaknesses?

f) What problems of technique does this author have that I can expect to face in my writing? How are they handled?

g) Is the writing quality commendable or deplorable? Are the characters real people? Are they sufficiently motivated in all their actions? Do they grow? Can I identify with them? Learn from them? Care about them?

h) Are the ideas in this book arranged in the best order to build toward a climax of thought?

i) Is this book scripturally sound? Does it honor God?

j) Which of the following words best describe the book? positive, negative, helpful, trivial, challenging, dull, colorful, stuffy, preachy, wordy, redundant, frivolous, meaty, accurate, sloppy, repulsive, cliché-ridden, trite, stimulating, reverent, fascinating, fresh, relevant, memorable

4. Do a Book Market study.

a) Go to a bookstore and browse through the shelves where your book will be displayed when it is published. Determine:

1) which publishers do the type of thing you are planning.

2) what books are already available in your subject area.

b) When you find a publisher that looks like a likely market, consult a marketing guide, send for current catalog of book offerings and a set of author's guidelines. Then, fill out a **Book Market Evaluation Sheet** (below) for each publisher you are considering.

BOOK MARKET EVALUATION SHEET ───────────

Name of publisher _____

Address _____

Editor(s) _____

Type of publisher: General book _____ General religious _____

Denomination _____ Organization _____

Target audiences: Ages _____ Education _____

Special interests _____

Number of books published per year _____

Types of books used: How-to __ Bible Study __ Issues __ Biographies __

Fiction __ Poetry __ Personal Experiences ____ Missionary ____ Youth ___

Devotional __ Commentaries/textbooks __ Reference _ Humor _ Gift __

Spirituality ___ Ministry ___ Women's ___ Other _____

Special requirements/slants/taboos _____

Royalty rates _____ Royalty payment _____

Proposal/query requirements _____

Comments: _____

Ideas for future submissions: _____

SUBMISSION RECORD

Item submitted   sent   rejected   accepted   comments

5. Get acquainted with the book publication process. It is similar to the **Idea To Publication** process for an article (see Lesson Eleven, Part One). Briefly, it consists of these steps:
   a) Idea and formulation of a theme
   b) Preliminary research
   c) Preparation of tentative outline
   d) Submission of a book proposal, which includes:
      1) Query letter
      2) Tentative Table of Contents
      3) Tentative paragraph outline (one-paragraph summary of each chapter)
      4) Two or three sample chapters (first chapter and one or two others, not necessarily in sequence)
   e) Go-ahead from an editor
      1) may be "on approval," meaning they want to see more before making a commitment.
      2) may be accompanied by a contract.
      3) In either case, the "go-ahead" letter will include editorial suggestions and deadlines.
   f) Further research, preparation, and submission of finished manuscript, following instructions from editor.
   g) Final acceptance and contract (if not included with *e* above). Usually accompanied by an author information form to be filled out by the author and used by editorial publicity departments in planning the promotion of book.
   h) Editing of the manuscript:
      1) By editor
      2) By author, as requested by editor
      3) *Galley* proofs prepared by editor and checked by both editor and author.
   i) Book publication. Happy day when you hold your bound volume in reverent hands, leaf through the pages, and ask, "Did I really write this?"
6. Study and practice all the special techniques of book writing. For this purpose, I recommend the following resources to guide you along the way:
   a) Books listed in the section, "Resources for Writers"
   b) Workshops and classes offered by local colleges and Adult Education
   c) Writers conferences, seminars, and workshops
   d) Critique groups of book writers.

You've done all of the above and you still feel compelled to write that book? Then begin by going on to the **Book Planning Worksheet** (below). Remember that book authoring is an awesome challenge.

Don't stretch and strain to find excuses why you should write a book. It's far too much work. Do all you can to get out of it. Only be sure to stay wide open to God's nudging and timing.

If God isn't in it, and you insist on doing it anyway, it will exhaust you and keep you from doing the thing He really wants you to do. If God is in it, you won't be able to get rid of the urge to do it, no matter how hard you try. When the book you couldn't resist begins to gestate and you entertain thoughts of aborting it, remember this: You can always count on the God who pushed you into it to bring you through the birth pangs into the indescribable joy of authorhood.

BOOK PLANNING WORKSHEET ——————————

1. Working Title:
2. General Subject:
3. Specific Subject:
4. Theme (What do I want to say?):
5. Purpose (What do I want to accomplish?):
6. Significance (What specific needs will it meet?):
7. Audience (Who am I trying to reach?):
8. Market (What publishers are likely to be interested?):
9. Uniqueness (What makes my idea different from other similar books already on the market?):
10. Qualifications (What makes me qualified to write it?):
11. Tentative Outline:
    a) Beginning
    b) Middle
    c) Ending
    d) Chapter divisions
12. Research to be done (See Research Planning Sheet, Lesson Seven, Part Two):
13. Book proposal (to include):
    a) Query Letter
    b) Table of Contents
    c) Chapter Summary Outline
    d) Sample Chapters:
       1) Chapter 1
       2) Chapter __
       3) Chapter __
14. List, in order of preference, publishers you plan to submit the proposal to.
15. Proposed Work Schedule

A Writer's Files

Some students once gave me a plaque that hangs over my desk and reads: "I finally got it all together, but I forgot where I put it."

After nearly three decades in this business, I still have problems keeping things straight. I've learned, however, that five different kinds of files do help, and I wouldn't try to function without them:

1. **IDEA FILE** (or notebook). (See Lesson One, Part Two)
2. **MARKET FILE**
   a) Organized in one of two ways. By:
   1) type of magazine (e.g., Christian education, women's, juvenile, etc.) or
   2) arrangement of magazines alphabetically, by title.
   b) Includes
   1) sample copies
   2) editorial guidelines
   3) market evaluation sheets.
3. **RESOURCE FILE**
   a) Alphabetical file, with separate folders for each subject (e.g., Alcohol, Families, Missions, etc.)
   b) Includes clippings, pamphlets, facts, ideas, observations, quotations, bibliographies, pictures, source addresses, snatches of text or journal entries you have already written.
   c) You may also use folders for sermon notes, poetry, examples of different forms of writing (e.g., personal experience stories, fiction stories, brochures)
4. **PROJECT FILE**
   a) One folder for each project you are working on or are considering working on. Arrange alphabetically by working title.

b) Each folder contains:
1) Notes
2) Bibliography
3) Correspondence concerning the project
4) Copy of submitted manuscript, along with filename if created and stored on a computer.
5) All drafts of the manuscript
6) Submission and financial records
7) Rejection slips (unless you are literally papering your walls with these!).

5. **CARD FILE** or **COMPUTER FILE**
You can use this file for at least four different kinds of entries. These may be separate card or computer files, or you may mix all kinds of entries in the same file, using a code (colors on cards; or letters/numbers in computer file).

a) **Market file**: addresses, with record of submissions.
b) **Bibliography file**: record of sources of research information, along with notations about when you read the material, where you found it, what was helpful about it, whether you have copies of any of its pages (if so, indicate where these may be found). (See sample below.)

Sample Bibliography Card

Gottschalk, Louis. *Understanding History (A Primer of Historical Method)*. ALFRED A. KNOPF: N.Y., 1961
Read 5/16/80- 6/10/80

SVPL*
907
G

*Sunnyvale Public Library.
If you own the book, record the word *Own* in this space,
perhaps with date of purchase.

c) **Address file:** people and organizations you deal with in your writing. Include dates of correspondence and any other notations of importance for quick reference, e.g., "Send new release on book publication" or "Hobby is collecting antique books" or "Knows president of N.Y. Historical Society."

d) **Data file**: good as a separate file for preserving short bits of research materials and keeping them accessible when you need them, usually while working on a specific project. (See samples below) I have found the following kinds of entries helpful:

1) Facts
2) Quotes
3) Ideas
4) Characters
5) Scenes
6) Dialogue
7) Other types of entries, to fit the project (e.g., chapter outlines or article outline segments, lists of technique items for easy review and evaluation).

Sample Data Cards

Quote
Anabaptism
"Reformers aimed to reform the old Church by the Bible; the radicals attempted to build a new church from the Bible."
Philip Schaff

The Anabaptist View of the Church
Frank Littell
Page xvii

Fact
Medicine
Remedies for sterility or impotence:
truffles
asparagus
eggs
girolle mushrooms
oysters
ambered wine

The Embarrassment of Riches
Simon Schama
Page 524

Organizing a Writers' Group

KINDS OF WRITERS GROUPS

1. **Christian Writers Club**: Loosely knit organization of Christians interested in writing. Includes inspirational sharing of market ideas, trends, speakers, and manuscript critiquing. Usually meets at the same time and place on a regular basis (normally monthly). May draw some nonwriters who wish they were writers, but rarely write. Majors on information, fellowship, and inspiration.
2. **Critique Group**: Small group of committed writers seriously interested in critical assistance for their never-ending flow of projects. May have a constant meeting place or may rotate in the homes of members. It is best to restrict membership to five or six, by invitation only. Emphasis is on actual working to improve manuscripts and skill level of members.
3. **Correspondence Group**: Round robin or computer sharing of serious publishing writers who submit manuscripts to each other by mail at regular intervals. May also share information, prayer needs, and techniques learned.
4. **Prayer Group**: Geographical groups who meet to pray for writers and editors and for the Christian publishing business worldwide. Not all members are writers or editors, but must have burden to pray for those who are. A couple of correspondence groups exist for this purpose. (See "Resources for Writers")

RECRUITING MEMBERS FOR A GROUP

1. Decide which kind of group you are interested in forming.
2. Some suggested methods for finding members:
    a) You may advertise in local churches or place announcements on bulletin boards at your local college or place of employment, if you work

for a Christian organization. **This method is not recommended for forming a critique group!** It will bring in some people who are not ready for critiquing by the rules and can be both disruptive to the group and destructive to individuals seeking help.

b) Talk to people at writers conferences and seminars.

c) Organize round robin or local critique group, taking in members on a limited basis and by personal invitation only. Some writers' clubs divide up their members into critique groups and keep them under able leadership of experienced writer/critics.

d) Form a nucleus of regularly publishing writers.

GUIDELINES FOR CONDUCTING A CRITIQUE GROUP

1. REMEMBER that you are neither a mutual admiration society nor a forum for showing off abilities and "setting others straight." A Christian writers' critique group is a body of Christian artists meeting to encourage and assist one another in the development of a mutual craft.

2. Ideally, your leader will be adept at teaching and leading group discussions with tact, firmness, and gentleness. A leader who hogs the time reading his/her own materials, and/or dishes out scathing denunciations of other members' work, will kill the group.

3. At the beginning of every session, give each member an opportunity to share the latest accomplishments and/or prayer needs directly related to writing. If necessary, time these reports. *Keep them short!*

4. Read and follow these guidelines for giving critiques in your sessions:

a) Plan for every writer to share, if possible.

1) If the group is large or your projects are complex, you may rotate so that not everyone reads at every meeting, but everyone gets a turn regularly. Or you may break into smaller groups to assure that this happens fairly.

2) Some groups restrict reading to a time or page limit. I can't do this, for I know no way to evaluate a manuscript without hearing it in its entirety (whole poem, article, book chapter or at least fairly self-contained section of a chapter).

3) The leader should encourage, but never coerce, shy members to participate. Sometimes it helps if you do the reading aloud for hesitant beginners.

b) As much as possible, writers should furnish copies of their work for members to read and make notes as the manuscripts are read. With poetry this is absolutely essential!

c) Let each writer read their manuscript aloud (or have someone else read it aloud), without interruption.

d) While a manuscript is being read, members should listen courteously and jot down comments to express later.

e) Give both general and specific reader comments. Begin with praises for what was done right. *You can **always** find at least one good thing about a manuscript!*

f) When corrections are needed, don't just call attention to errors, but also suggest alternatives that will correct and/or improve the work. At the same time, refrain from rewriting the other person's manuscript, imposing your own style on it.

g) Never allow one person to monopolize the discussion.

h) Balance honesty with love in critiquing a work.

i) Be sensitive to the feelings of writers and offer criticism with caution, according to what you feel a writer is ready to receive. Don't expect the same level of excellence from both beginners and experienced writers. If you insist on correcting every problem you find in a beginner's manuscript, you will overwhelm, discourage, and destroy. Help members to learn at their own speed.

j) Never attack the writer's abilities or person. Merely suggest ideas for improvement in the manuscripts and technique.

5. Include sharing of markets, books, technical helps, other shop talk, and prayer requests. In the group that has met in my home for years, we take time to pray for each individual's special needs which impact their writing ministry. It's always a struggle to remember that we are a writing group, not a prayer meeting. But we are committed to serving as a body of believers in ministry and the rewards have amply justified the effort.

6. Strive and pray for a unified, loving spirit in your group. Your goal is not competitive, nor is it simply to turn out salable manuscripts. Rather, it should be to accomplish "the praise of the glory of his grace" (Ephesians 1:6, KJV). This can only happen when you guard a nurturing atmosphere and concern for each member's work and stage of personal and technical growth.

> *Love is patient, love is kind, and is not jealous;*
> *love does not brag and is not arrogant,*
> *does not act unbecomingly;*
> *it does not seek its own, is not provoked,*
> *does not take into account a wrong suffered,...*
> *bears all things,*
> *believes all things,*
> *hopes all things,*
> *endures all things.*
> *Love never fails.*
> 1 Corinthians 13:4-8a (NASB)

Insights on Essays

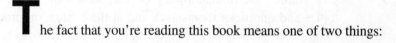

The fact that you're reading this book means one of two things:

1. A school counselor has warned you that the essay "can play a significant role in the admission decision, and so you'd better take it seriously."

2. A friend who is already working on his or her essays has suggested that you "go buy one of those books that includes a bunch of essays to get some ideas."

Both the counselor and the friend are right, but you're probably still worried about all of this—for one (or more) of three reasons:

1. Your GPA isn't spectacular, and you doubt that even a great essay will get you into your first-choice college.

2. You don't consider yourself a "good" writer or a "creative" writer.

3. You believe you've lived such an ordinary life that you have nothing interesting, important, or unique to say to the admission committee.

Wrong, wrong, and wrong! Okay, there's nothing you can do about your GPA (except to improve your grades in the future). Let's concentrate on what you *can* do. So you're not another Hemingway or Twain. Does this mean you have to settle for a college admission essay that is just "okay" or even "pretty good"? Absolutely not. Writing effective essays does not require creative genius, divine inspiration, or a high I.Q. It does not require that you've traveled, volunteered to further social causes, dined with well-known influential people, or looked death in the face. All it requires is some self-knowledge, time, and effort.

Part 1 of this book is crammed with practical, useful tools to help you generate ideas and craft a masterpiece. Don't feel, however, that you have to follow every piece of advice included here. These tips are meant to help you get started; they are not intended as hard-and-fast rules for writing admission essays.

Before the brainstorming begins, let's look at the essay topics and questions themselves and at the evaluation process.

ESSAY TOPICS ON THE "COMMON APPLICATION"

The Common Application is a standard application form designed to simplify and streamline the college application process. The Common Application is the recommended form of more than 240 selective colleges and universities, many of which use the Common Application exclusively. The Personal Statement section of the Common Application reads as follows:

This personal statement helps us become acquainted with you as an individual in ways different from courses, grades, test scores, and other objective data. It will demonstrate your ability to organize thoughts to express yourself. We are looking for an essay that will help us know you better as a person and as a student. Please write an essay (250–500 words) on a topic of your choice or on one of the options listed below. You may attach your essay on separate sheets (same size, please).

1. Evaluate a significant experience, achievement, risk you have taken, or ethical dilemma you have faced and its impact on you.

2. Discuss some issue of personal, local, national, or international concern and its importance to you.

3. Indicate a person who has had a significant influence on you, and describe that influence.

4. Describe a character in fiction, an historical figure, or a creative work (as in art, music, science, etc.) that has had an influence on you, and explain that influence.

5. Topic of your choice*

The Common Application is available at the official Common Application Group Web site (www.commonapp.org). Some schools accepting the Common Application require that you print out and complete a hard copy for submission. But most schools accepting the Common Application permit you to fill out the application form (including the essay) online, and then submit it to the school over the Internet—all via the Common Application Web site.

Even among the schools that don't use the Common Application, some variation on one or more of these four topics is often used. Nevertheless, a wide variety of additional essay topics and questions also appear on college applications. The essay topics vary so widely that it would be futile to try to list them all or to categorize them here. Besides, there is no best way to respond to specific types of questions and topics (regardless of what you might read elsewhere). The key is to follow general guidelines and to discover your own style and voice that you can apply to any kind of essay.

---

* © 2001, Common Application Group. Used with permission.

THE ROLE OF THE ESSAY IN THE ADMISSION PROCESS

✎ HOW IMPORTANT IS MY ESSAY IN THE ADMISSION DECISION?

It depends. Except at the most selective schools, if your GPA and SAT scores are both remarkably high, then as long as you don't write something patently stupid or offensive in your essays, your GPA and SAT scores will probably convince the admission committee at the school to admit you. On the other hand, if a particular school is a long-shot for you, then even a great essay will probably not in itself persuade the admission committee to admit you. The fact is this: The closer you are to the borderline, the more significant a role your essay will play in the admission decision.

✎ CAN I BE ASSURED THAT SOMEONE AT THE COLLEGE WILL READ MY ESSAY(S)?

Most colleges will tell you essentially: "Assuming that you have submitted a complete application and have met our application deadline, your essay(s) will be read by at least one person in our office." Generally speaking, this is true. However, smaller schools—especially private liberal arts colleges—with small applicant pools tend to pay greater attention than larger colleges and universities to applicants' essays. Also, at some schools with large applicant pools, essays by applicants whose GPA and SAT scores fail to meet minimum or threshold requirements might go unread.

✎ WHO WILL READ AND EVALUATE MY ESSAY(S)?

Procedures vary among schools. Typically, however, one *admission officer* will read your essay(s) and write an evaluation. Admission officers are typically graduates, or *alumni*, of the school for which they work and are hired to evaluate applications; they do not, however, make final admission decisions. If you remain a viable candidate after the first "read," your essay(s) will then be scrutinized more closely by another admission officer or perhaps by the admission director or assistant director. Some schools (particularly small liberal arts colleges) will subject your essays to further scrutiny by circulating your file among members of an admission committee comprised of perhaps five to seven people (admission officials, faculty members, and possibly students).

✎ HOW DO SCHOOLS EVALUATE MY ESSAYS?

Evaluation methods vary somewhat among schools. Some schools, particularly larger institutions that process many applications, use a multiple-scoring system in which each essay receives separate scores for content, style, and mechanics. Other schools take a more holistic approach, relying on written comments by evaluators as well as dialogue among members of the admission committee.

10 STEPS TO AN AWESOME ADMISSION ESSAY

1. LEARN MORE ABOUT YOURSELF

College admission personnel want to get to know you personally through your essays. How can they get to know who you really are if you yourself are not really sure? Here are some self-discovery tools and techniques that will help ensure that the schools are meeting the *real* you through your essays.

✎ INTERVIEW YOUR FRIENDS AND RELATIVES

This can be a tough but very useful exercise. Try the following five questions; encourage your interview subjects to be brutally honest, and get ready to eat some humble pie:

1. How have you described me to people who haven't met me?

2. What's the best thing anyone has ever told you about me?

3. What's the worst thing anyone has ever told you about me?

4. What do you think is my most unusual or unique character trait?

5. What was your initial impression of me when you first met me? How has that changed?

✎ RECORD YOUR DREAMS

Nothing is more sincere and personal, and nothing is more unique and unusual, than a dream. You'll be amazed at the essay ideas you can dream up while you sleep!

✎ WRITE DOWN YOUR THOUGHTS AND FEELINGS ABOUT ISSUES THAT ARE MOST PERSONAL AND IMMEDIATE

Let's face it: Most 16- and 17-year olds are usually not as concerned with geopolitics and medieval literature as they are about more personal issues such as

- ✓ Self-esteem (approval and validation of self, ideas, and values)
- ✓ Identity
- ✓ Independence from parents
- ✓ Academic and extra-curricular success
- ✓ Popularity and acceptance by a peer group
- ✓ Sexuality, physical appearance, and attractiveness
- ✓ Loyalty, trust, and honesty

Set aside some time every day to be alone and reflect on your own thoughts and feelings about these issues. If you keep a diary or journal, excerpts from these writings may very well provide the genesis of a highly effective essay.

✎ MAKE AN APPOINTMENT WITH YOUR HIGH SCHOOL COUNSELOR TO TALK ABOUT LIFE IN GENERAL

Tell your counselor that you need assistance in learning more about yourself—who you really are and what you really want out of life. Be certain that you meet with a counselor you can trust to keep your conversation strictly confidential.

2. DO SOME SERIOUS BRAINSTORMING

Make the following exercises part of your daily routine for a month, and you'll be bursting at the seams with unique ideas for essays!

✎ RECORD OBSERVATIONS IN A "BELIEVE IT OR NOT" NOTEBOOK

Seemingly ordinary events can be quite interesting when viewed through a creative lens. Record interesting sights, bits of conversation, and events that you observe firsthand—at home, at school, and elsewhere. Try to see the unusual in the ordinary. Two masters of this art are George Carlin and Jerry Seinfeld, both of whom have a knack for finding something absurd about everyday happenings to which anyone can relate.

✎ BECOME A KEEN OBSERVER OF HUMAN BEHAVIOR

Study the following behavior in people around you:

✓ Introversion (shyness) and extroversion

✓ Aggressiveness, assertiveness, and passivity

✓ Friendliness and unfriendliness

✓ Various kinds of intelligence, talent, and skill

✓ Competitiveness and cooperation

✓ Self-affirming behavior and self-defeating behavior

✎ READ THE EDITORIAL SECTION OF YOUR LOCAL NEWSPAPER

Newspaper editorial pages are chock-full of ideas for issue-related essays. These pages will also serve up good examples of effective as well as ineffective writing styles.

✎ SCAN THE MAGAZINE RACK AT THE LOCAL LIBRARY FOR PERIODICALS THAT LOOK INTERESTING TO YOU

Avoid the most popular titles, such as *Time* and *Newsweek*. Instead, take a look at periodicals such as *The New Yorker*.

✎ CHECK OUT COLLEGE-RELATED INTERNET RESOURCES

Web sites devoted to college admission are springing up like weeds these days. Check them out, and download everything you can about admission essays. Also, you might find discussions about college admission essays on various Internet bulletin boards.

✎ SURF THE WEB FOR INTERESTING ARTICLES AND ESSAYS

Make note of potential topics and ideas for your essays, then use some of the Web's powerful search engines to find related Web sites. Also, don't forget to check out the many online magazines and periodicals, or *zines*, available on the Web.

✎ READ ESSAYS BY THE GREAT ESSAYISTS

Perhaps you're a bit insecure about your writing ability. Most great writers—as well as great artists and musicians—get to be great by emulating (but not mimicking) the masters. Take this as your cue. Go to the library and read essays by great essayists. After two hours in the library, you'll be oozing with inspiration—guaranteed. Use your favorite writer's style as a starting point for developing your own, as long as the style feels natural to you. Here's a list of writers to get you started:

✓ Some contemporary essayists:
  Calvin Trillin
  Anna Quindlen
  Dave Berry

✓ A few modern essayists:
  John Updike
  H.L. Mencken
  Tom Wolfe
  George Orwell

✓ Some not-so-modern essayists:
  Henry Thoreau
  Ralph Waldo Emerson
  Jonathan Swift

✓ Two writers who write about writing:
  William Zinsser
  E.B. White

✎ TAKE A FRESH LOOK AT ESSAYS THAT YOU HAVE ALREADY WRITTEN

Dust off those old essays you wrote for your English and creative writing classes. One of these essays may provide the genesis or inspiration for a great college admission essay. Resist the temptation, however, to take the easy way out by simply using one of these essays as your admission essay. Admission officers can smell recycled school papers a mile away!

3. CHECK OUT THE COLLEGE'S OWN RESOURCES FOR ESSAY IDEAS

Colleges themselves are great places to start gathering information and ideas for your essays. However, many applicants never think to look there. Here's a checklist for you to make sure you take advantage of all that a college has to offer you as an applicant.

✎ READ SEVERAL ISSUES OF THE SCHOOL NEWSPAPER

You'll learn what local and regional issues are important to the administration, faculty, and students. Certain newsworthy school events or happenings might strike you as particularly interesting, unique, shocking, or praiseworthy. Consider writing about such an issue or event in your essay for that school.

✎ READ THE ALUMNI PUBLICATIONS PRODUCED BY THE SCHOOL

Ask yourself: What values seem to be important to the administration and to the trustees? What image is the school attempting to convey? What are the school's policies and attitudes? What alumni accomplishments is the school touting? Perhaps these values, policies, and accomplishments are worth addressing in your essay.

✎ TOUR THE CAMPUS WITH YOUR EYES WIDE OPEN

Observe the architecture, the sculptures, and other artwork around the campus. Read the plaques and engravings on, in, and around the buildings. Walk around the neighborhood surrounding the campus looking for essay nuggets in your path. If you can't visit the school in person, take an online tour of the school or obtain an information video from the school, if one is available. (Keep in mind, however, that schools' Web sites and videos are marketing tools as well as informational resources, so they may not present a completely objective picture of the school.)

✎ INVESTIGATE THE SCHOOL'S HISTORY

You'll be amazed at the inventive essay ideas that emerge. Here are just a few investigative questions to get you started:

✓ What were the political and economic circumstances surrounding the founding of the school? What were the founders' ideals and educational philosophies, and has the school moved away from its initial educational mission?

✓ Did the school ever serve as the subject, locale, or backdrop for an important historical event? What does that event mean to you?

✓ Who are the school's most famous alumni (or dropouts)? What are their accomplishments and impact upon you, the school, and society? Why did those individuals attend the college, and what kind of students were they?

✎ TALK TO CURRENT STUDENTS

Go to the central meeting place on campus, find some students who are hanging out (you won't have any trouble finding them), and strike up a conversation. Ask them about life in the dormitory, fraternity, or sorority. Ask them what attracted them to the school initially and whether their initial perceptions about the school have changed. Ask them if they know any tales about legendary school pranks. You're sure to walk away with all sorts of essay ideas!

✎ READ WHAT THE ADMISSION APPLICATION SAYS ABOUT THE ESSAYS

A surprisingly large number of applicants ignore the directions and guidelines for essay writing that are spelled out in the school's application. Be sure you're not one of these students! Many schools include not only directions but also advice for writing the essay.

✎ CONTACT THE ADMISSION STAFF WITH UNANSWERED QUESTIONS ABOUT THE ESSAY

After you have read the application materials thoroughly, if any of the guidelines (concerning topic scope, page length, etc.) are still unclear, contact the school and ask for clarification. Don't be afraid to communicate with the school's admission staff yourself.

✎ VISIT THE SCHOOL'S WEB SITE

The Internet is probably the quickest and least expensive means of gathering information about colleges. Virtually all colleges and universities now make available online their school catalogues as well as admission policies, procedures, applications, and other information.

4. AVOID OVERUSED IDEAS: SEEK OUT OVERLOOKED IDEAS

Okay, you've just sat down with pen and paper (or mouse and monitor) to respond to a particular essay question. A brilliant, attention-grabbing, original idea immediately pops into your head. Before hastily committing your flash of genius to paper and rushing it to the admission committee, think again. Chances are that your initial original idea is anything but original. In this section, we'll list some of the most overused ideas and suggest some alternative and fresh approaches.

✎ ESSAYS ABOUT PERSONAL RELATIONSHIPS AND INFLUENCES

In choosing a subject for an essay about a personal relationship or about someone you know personally who has influenced you, in addition to the more obvious choices, such as members of your immediate family or your best friend, consider subjects such as:

✓ Your favorite teacher

✓ Your coach

✓ Distant relatives (cousins, nieces, nephews) from other times or other places

✓ Your arch-rival at school

✓ A student at school who is experiencing academic or social problems

✓ A neighbor

✓ Penpals (or cyberfriends)

✓ A member of a friend's family

Don't write about your dog Spot or cat Fluffy. Admission officers have read far too many essays about family pets!

✎ ESSAYS ABOUT ISSUES

If asked to write about an issue of societal significance, keep in mind that the following issues are discussed by many applicants:

✗ The environment

✗ World peace

✗ Prejudice and discrimination

✗ Drugs

✗ Crime

If your personal experience or conviction strongly leads you to write on one of these topics, by all means go ahead. Otherwise, consider more neglected issues such as these:

✓ Individual rights (e.g., right to die, AIDS, abortion, gun control, free speech)

✓ Consumerism and materialism

✓ Fairness, justice, and equity (but please don't mention O.J. Simpson)

✓ Free trade among nations

✓ Internet issues (e.g., privacy, alienation, education, commerce)

✎ ESSAYS ABOUT YOUR EXPERIENCES OR ACTIVITIES OR ABOUT SIGNIFICANT EVENTS IN YOUR LIFE

Unless you have something highly intimate, unique, or creative to share with the reader about the experience, think again before you use any of the following as the focal point of your essay:

✗ The college admission process (especially the SAT and essay writing)

✗ Your big trip to some faraway place, especially if you focus on:

How it enhanced your cultural awareness

How yucky the food was

How it taught you to accept people who were different

The *Wizard of Oz* angle (i.e., there's no place like home)

✗ Wilderness and survival experiences; your exciting Outward Bound trek no doubt taught you to face your fears, to meet new challenges, and to rise to the occasion, but hundreds of other applicants have regaled admission officers with similar experiences

✗ Winning or losing the big game, election, or other competition, if you use one of these tired themes:

  It's not whether you win or lose

  I now have greater self-confidence

  I learned the importance of teamwork

  I learned that my true talents lie elsewhere

✗ How all your discipline and hard work paid off in the end (the *Little Engine That Could* essay)

✗ Summer camp

✗ A part-time job ("I learned more than I ever could have in school")

✗ Your most unforgettable experience

Look elsewhere for personal experiences to share with the admission committee; for example:

✓ A seemingly ordinary school field trip or outing with friends or family that turned into an unexpected adventure or self-defining event

✓ A song, a poem, novel, or other serious literary or artistic work that made a genuine and deep impact on the way you look at yourself, others, the world around you, and life in general

✓ The time you received an unexpected gift from an unexpected source, or the time you spontaneously gave of yourself to someone or something

✓ A white lie, an off-the-cuff insulting remark, or a discourtesy (either yours or someone else's) that helped you to grow and mature in your understanding of yourself and others

✓ A contribution or accomplishment of yours motivated not by potential external reward but by some other force or reason

✓ An informal social situation that you replay over and over in your mind because it holds more meaning for you than seemingly more important events, such as holidays, weddings, or proms

✓ Those times when teachers or other authority figures let their guard down for you, enabling you to approach them as an equal and as a friend

✎ ESSAYS ABOUT YOUR OWN PERSONAL QUALITIES

If the school's application calls for you to write about your own character, personality, likes, dislikes, or values, try to avoid these trite ideas and themes:

✗ Lists of your favorite things or least-favorite things (please spare the admission officers your "sung to the tune of 'My Favorite Things'" masterpiece)

✗ Your determination and tenacity; don't write about how you always get what you want or accomplish what you seek out to do

✗ How diverse you are in your interests and endeavors (the "Renaissance man" essay)

Instead, look inward at your quirky, seemingly less attractive, or downright negative traits. Don't be hesitant to expose a weakness or admit your fallibility. For example, don't be reluctant to talk about:

✓ Those little habits of yours that sometimes annoy those around you

✓ That time you really put your foot in your mouth

✓ A personal possession to which you have grown irrationally attached

✓ Particular study habits that you would like to change

✓ Your unusual awkwardness in certain social situations

5. OBSERVE THESE DO'S AND DON'TS FOR THEME AND CONTENT

✓ **DO** write an essay that only you could honestly write. If it's possible that the reader will read anything similar from any other applicant, go back to the drawing board.

✓ **DO** convey a positive message overall. Cynicism will not score points with the admission committee.

✓ **DO** strive for depth, not breadth. Focus on one event or idea rather than trying to cover an entire subject. Think personal and anecdotal.

✓ **DO** reject your first idea or angle. It's probably been used a million times.

✓ **DO** be interesting but more important, be yourself. Convey your true and genuine thoughts and feelings; don't try to portray yourself as someone with interests, values, and opinions that aren't really yours.

✓ **DO** write about what you know and have observed or experienced firsthand, *not* about things that are beyond your personal development as a teenager. Book knowledge or other secondhand information does not convey to the reader any sense of who you are.

✓ **DO** write about something you feel strongly about. If you write on a topic about which you have little interest or knowledge, your lack of sincerity and enthusiasm will show in your writing.

✓ **DO** write about other people as well as about yourself. We are defined as individuals largely in terms of our experiences with others, and acknowledging this through your essay will help ensure that you don't appear overly self-centered.

✓ **DO** be experiential, but avoid too much imagery. Relate to the reader the full scope of an experience—sights, sounds, and perhaps even smells. Be careful, however, not to overuse imagery; otherwise, the result may be a forced, unnatural style that gives the reader the impression that you are trying too hard to be creative.

✗ **DON'T** let others—especially your parents—decide for you what to write. Feel free to brainstorm with others for ideas, but don't ask: "What should I write about?"

✗ **DON'T** try to sell yourself or prove anything by convincing the reader how great you are, how smart you are, or how accomplished you are. Your definitive theories and brilliant solutions to global problems will not impress the reader. Admit it: You have many more questions than answers at this point in your life. Use your essay as an opportunity to wonder about life, to pose thoughtful questions, and to probe and investigate, *not* to tell the reader "the way it is."

✗ **DON'T** try to write an important or scholarly essay. A well-researched essay that shows off your knowledge of a particular academic subject tells the reader nothing about you. The reader will only suspect that your essay is actually a recycled term paper.

✗ **DON'T** try to guess what the admission committee wants you to write. This approach will result in a "safe" essay that will fall flat.

✗ **DON'T** rehash what the reader already knows about you. Don't reiterate accomplishments or activities that are already mentioned elsewhere in your application.

✗ **DON'T** appear overly idealistic. World peace and a clean environment are worthy ideals, but avoid coming across as preachy or fanatic. There are always at least two sides to every controversial issue, so recognize the merits of all sides. Otherwise, you might sound a bit naive.

✗ **DON'T** waste your essay opportunity to explain blemishes or deficiencies in your application. A low grade, a low SAT score, or an absence of extracurricular activities is not a worthy subject for discussion in your essay. If you must defend a blemish in your record, contact the school and ask (anonymously) if you can attach a separate (and brief) explanation as an addendum to your application. As an alternative, ask your college counselor to clarify these points in his or her recommendation letter.

✗ **DON'T** write anything that might embarrass the reader or make him or her feel uncomfortable. There's nothing wrong with discussing sensitive topics such as substance abuse, sexuality, spirituality, religious beliefs, and political views. Just be sure to treat the subject gingerly, avoid generalizations, and use a respectful tone. Otherwise, you may put off or even offend the reader.

✗ **DON'T** write an essay that reads like a newspaper editorial. The schools welcome your opinions, but don't get on a soap box and appear overly critical of other viewpoints.

✗ **DON'T** even think about mentioning popular television shows, movies, musicians, or actors, regardless of how significant they are to you; and please don't mention any Dr. Seuss book. (The wastebaskets in admission offices fill to the brim every fall with Dr. Suess essays.)

6. WRITE, WRITE, AND WRITE SOME MORE

Anyone who has ever sat down to write an open-ended essay has experienced some degree of writer's block or paralysis. Sometimes the biggest problem is just getting the words flowing. Here are some useful tips that will help get your pencil (or keyboard keys) moving.

✎ TRY SOME STREAM-OF-CONSCIOUSNESS SPEED DRILLS

Pick a topic (any topic), then fill up a piece of paper with words as fast as you possibly can in a stream-of-consciousness fashion. You may find it helpful to impose a time limit on yourself. Don't worry about content, style, or grammar; just loosen up that pencil!

✎ KEEP ALL YOUR DRAFTS, EVEN YOUR ROUGHEST ONES

As you write first drafts, don't worry about grammar. Keep all your drafts, even the roughest ones. Writing is like any other creative endeavor—for some people the initial effort produces the best result, while for others a superior product results from a long process of crafting and fine-tuning.

✎ START WITH THE FOUR COMMON APPLICATION QUESTIONS

Carry around a notepad and jot down your thoughts on these topics as you think of them, without trying to organize them. Stimulate your thinking even more by bouncing your thoughts off others during your everyday conversations; as soon as possible, jot down the ideas that emerged during those conversations. You might discover your best essay right there on your notepad.

✎ EXPRESS YOUR IDEAS AND OPINIONS FREELY ON THE INTERNET

Post your writing anonymously to appropriate issue-related newsgroups and bulletin boards. This might help you overcome writer's block, and you might obtain some useful feedback that will stimulate more ideas and help you to fine-tune your essays. However, don't give away your ideas or essays by posting them on college admission bulletin boards.

✎ KNOW WHEN YOU ARE FINISHED

Don't write forever! At some point, leave well enough alone, print out your essay, and submit it. Bear in mind that beyond a certain point, additional editing, fine-tuning, and revising will probably result in an essay that is well-written but lacking in character and distinctiveness—not the end result that you want!

7. IMPRESS THEM WITH YOUR STYLE . . . BUT DON'T RESORT TO GIMMICKS

Your writing style—format, structure, syntax, tone, word choice, and the like—may play just as important a role as content in the school's overall evaluation of your essay. Strive to develop a style that is natural, somewhat informal, and distinctly your own. Here are some more specific guidelines.

✎ STRUCTURE AND FORMAT OF THE ESSAY

Each school will, of course, impose its own guidelines and restrictions as to essay length. Otherwise, the format and structure is left largely to the writer. Here are five important points to keep in mind:

1. Short essays are generally preferable to long ones. An essay that is concise and to the point will be appreciated by the reader. Do not take this advice too far, however. Be careful not to sacrifice substance or cut your mes-

sage short merely for brevity's sake. (You will notice some effective longer essays in Part 2 of this book.) Also, one-word and one-sentence essays have been tried a thousand times but have not worked once.

2. Use logical, frequent paragraph breaks at points where you think the reader could use a break. Don't limit yourself to the five-paragraph essay format you learned in English class.

3. Avoid poetry unless it's the only way to get your message across and you are quite good at it. Sonnets, limericks, haiku, and "sung to the tune of . . ." essays have been tried many times, so think again before abandoning good-old prose.

4. Drawings, cartoons, and other visual devices are best left to serious artists. If drawing or graphic arts is your passion and potential career, by all means present yourself through this medium to the college's art department (especially if you're really good). Otherwise, don't.

5. So you want to be a lawyer someday? Please don't write an essay in the form of a contract or court document. Is it your dream to become a physician? Don't write your essay in the form of prescription. Got the general idea?

✎ FINDING AN APPROPRIATE AND GENUINE STYLE AND TONE

In an attempt to get noticed, don't resort to an extreme or gimmicky writing style that doesn't reflect your true "voice." The appropriate tone and style should emerge naturally from the message you wish to convey. Here are five specific points of advice to bear in mind:

1. Strive to write in a style that reads like a telephone conversation with a friend, without all the "uhm"s, "like"s, and "you know"s.

2. Don't try too hard to be funny. It's okay to be lighthearted and to show a dry and subtle humor about your topic, but don't write a humorous essay *per se*. No puns, please!

3. Be forceful and opinionated, but don't insult or offend. A bit of irreverence in your tone and attitude is perfectly acceptable—in fact, the reader will find it refreshing. However, an overly flippant or disrespectful tone might suggest that you don't take the essay or the admission process very seriously.

4. Avoid whining, complaining, or appearing bitter, sarcastic, angry, caustic, boastful, or aggressive.

5. Avoid coming across as overly humble.

✎ THE ALL-IMPORTANT OPENING SENTENCES

First impressions are important. Strive to engage the reader immediately with an opener that will make him or her want to read on. Avoid trite and hackneyed introductions—specifically:

✗ Don't introduce yourself to the admission committee—for example, "Hello, my name is . . ."

✗ Don't ask the reader's permission to tell him or her about yourself—for example, "Please permit me to discuss my . . ."

✗ Stay away from term-paper style introductory paragraphs. Don't reiterate the topic or question or itemize the points you will make in subsequent paragraphs. In other words, break all the rules you learned in class for writing term papers.

Okay, then how *should* you begin your essay? Try taking your cue from comedians who know how to capture an audience's interest right from the start. Tune in to some stand-up comedy shows on television and take notes. Here are some opening angles to consider:

✓ An enigmatic statement that makes the reader wonder to what or to whom you are referring

✓ An obscure quotation (avoid popular quotations or quotations from famous people)

✓ A thoughtful question

✓ A trivial observation that anyone can relate to but that nobody else would ever think to mention in an essay

✓ A paradox

✓ A gross generalization

✓ Someone else's opinion or theory

✓ A confession

✓ An overly obvious statement

✎ ESSAY ENDINGS

Notice that we use the term "ending" here instead of "conclusion" or "summary." This is because conclusions and summaries are for term papers, not for your admission essay. Here are a few DO's and DON'Ts to ensure that your essay ends with a bang, not a bomb:

✓ **DO** provide closure—a sense that you have provided the reader with bookends to your essay or that you have come full circle by the end of your essay.

✓ **DO** use the final sentences to end any suspense and to answer any question that you might have posed earlier in the essay.

✓ **DO** use short, forceful sentences to end your essay.

✗ **DON'T** address the admission committee or ask them to admit you.

✗ **DON'T** use words like "finally," "in sum," or "in conclusion."

✗ **DON'T** repeat or sum up in any way.

✗ **DON'T** end your essay with a quotation.

✎ INCLUDING A TITLE FOR YOUR ESSAY

Is it a good idea to precede your essay with a brief, attention-grabbing title? The use of titles is acceptable but superfluous in the eyes of the reader, who is far more concerned with the content of the essay itself. Go ahead and use a title if you think it would help communicate your message or if you have a great idea for a title that you can't resist using; otherwise, don't. By the way, some of the essays in Part 2 of this book originally included titles, although most did not. (The essay titles are not included in Part 2.)

✎ WORD CHOICE

Words are the building blocks for communicating ideas. Without a strong foundation, your message will be ineffective. While word choice depends on your personal writing style and your message, there are certain kinds of words you should avoid in your essay.

✗ **AVOID** words that are used over and over on resumes, in job descriptions, and in books of virtues. These words are guaranteed to result in a dry, dull style and a potentially boastful tone. Here are just a few examples:

responsibility	goal
interact	role
develop	integrity
leadership	excellence
interpersonal	

✗ **AVOID** slang and currently popular buzz phrases. You'll be "dissed" and "brutalized" by the admission committee, so write your essay in this style—NOT!

✗ **AVOID** superfluous words and phrases, including "courtroom" rhetoric, waffle words, needless self-references, and transition words. Here are a few examples:

rhetoric:
clearly
obviously
unquestionably

waffle words:
somewhat
rather
quite
perhaps

self-references:
I think
I believe
my feeling is that

transition words:
first, second, third, finally
thus, in conclusion
moreover
however
the next point

✗ **AVOID** technical, scientific, and obscure "SAT-style" words. A plethora of garish periphrasis may come across as haughty or supercilious. Get the idea?

✎ STYLISTIC DEVICES—DO'S AND DON'TS

All great writers have their favorite literary devices that distinguish their writing. Here are some devices to help make your essay shine, along with some others to avoid:

✓ **DO** use analogies (metaphors and similes) to help convey your message, but don't overdo it.

✓ **DO** incorporate dialogue into your essay, but think twice about using a screenplay approach (unless you plan to major in the theater arts).

✓ **DO** use more short sentences than long ones. Don't take this to an extreme, however. Mix up sentence length so that your essay flows naturally and rhythmically when read aloud.

✓ **DO** use logical paragraph breaks to provide a visual break for the reader and to indicate a change in direction, train of thought, or idea. Don't set off any one sentence as a separate paragraph, except for dialogue or for dramatic impact.

✓ **DO** use the active voice instead of the passive voice. In most cases, the active voice is preferred. Here's an example of each:

> *(active)* The applicant wrote an outstanding essay.

> *(passive)* A less-than-outstanding essay was written by the applicant.

✗ **DON'T** tell the reader explicitly, in effect: "I am a unique and interesting person." Instead, let the reader glean this from your interesting and unique essay.

✗ **DON'T** mimic or parody a well-known writer or literary work. If the writer or work is unfamiliar to the reader, your essay might look pretty silly! Worse yet, if the reader knows and admires the author's work, you might offend the reader.

✗ **DON'T** be a dummy by dabbling in dumb alliterations.

✗ **DON'T** start too many sentences with the word "I."

✗ **DON'T** use the phrase "a lot of." A lot of applicants use "a lot of" a lot of times. There are a lot of other choices—such as "many," "numerous," and "significant."

✗ **DON'T** necessarily write entirely in complete sentences. A complete sentence includes both a subject and a predicate. Remember? The previous sentence wasn't really a sentence, was it? Nevertheless, it could be quite acceptable in an essay if it flows naturally and is useful for emphasis or stylistic impact.

8. AVOID CARELESS ERRORS AND GRAMMATICAL BLUNDERS

The schools will not penalize you for one or two minor mechanical or grammatical errors. Glaring or frequent errors may, however, adversely affect your chances of admission. Above all, make sure that you heed the following two pieces of advice:

1. There's no excuse for spelling errors in your essay! Don't just run your essay through a spell-checking program. Spell-checkers don't catch words that may be spelled correctly in some other context but not as they are used in your essay. Four example, the first word in this sentence would slip past a spell-checker, wouldn't it?!

2. You'd better get the name of the school right! Otherwise, you'll insult the reader and appear careless and sloppy. Is the school a "College" or "University"? Is it "University of . . ." or ". . . University"? Have you inadvertently used the name of another school to which you are sending a similar essay?

As for grammar, there are literally thousands of grammatical blunders that you might potentially commit in writing your essay. It would be futile to attempt to cover the rules of grammar here. The best way to ensure that your essay is grammatically correct is to refer to a comprehensive grammar guide. Here are three good ones:

1. *Prentice Hall Reference Guide to Grammar and Usage*, by Muriel Harris, published by Prentice Hall.

2. *Harbrace College Handbook*, by John C. Hodges, et al., 12th Edition, Published by Harcourt Brace Johanovich, College & School Division.

3. *MLA Handbook for Writers of Research Papers*, by Joseph Gibaldi, 6th Edition, published by the Modern Language Association of America.

Also, don't forget about another invaluable resource: your high school English teacher.

9. OBTAIN USEFUL FEEDBACK AND FINE-TUNE YOUR ESSAY

Here are 10 tips and techniques to help you obtain useful feedback that will result in the most effective possible essay:

1. When showing your essay to others, avoid asking, "Do you like it?" Instead, ask something like: "If you didn't know me, what would you say about the person who wrote this essay?"

2. Set aside each draft for several days, then go back to it. It's quite possible that a particular point or idea that you thought was so brilliant or clever one day will come across as corny or downright inane a week later.

3. Post bits and pieces of rough drafts to topically relevant Internet newsgroups and bulletin boards, then check back for reactions. Don't let on, however, that your posted articles pertain to your college admission essays.

4. Try to imagine that you're flipping television channels, and on one channel someone is reading your essay aloud. Would you change channels, or would you be

intrigued enough to stay tuned to that channel to hear the rest of the story?

5. People who you ask for feedback probably have not worked in the admission field, so take their advice with a grain of salt!

6. Join or start an essay writing club at your high school. Feedback from classmates can be just as valuable as feedback from teachers and other adults.

7. Don't ask too many people to read your essay. Your own voice might get lost as a result of your critics' comments and suggestions.

8. Although it may be painful, don't be reluctant to discard an essay and start from scratch. If you've revised it again and again but are still not pleased with it, you're probably on the wrong track and need a fresh, new approach.

9. Converse with others about the topic of your essay, without letting on that you are relating its substance. You'll get far more candid responses with this approach.

10. If others describe your essay as cute, humorous, or clever, go back to your word processor and try to be less cute, humorous, or clever. After reading your essay, do others describe you as: mature, responsible, organized, hard-working, accomplished, determined, principled, or nice? If so, you're probably on the wrong track. Here are some key feedback words and phrases that indicate you are on the *right* track with your essay: delightful, wonderful, affectionate, warm, lighthearted, savvy, elegant, insightful, sensitive, fun, thoughtful, genuine, vivid, wow, I'd like to meet . . . , I can really relate. . . .

10. PACKAGE AND PRESENT YOUR ESSAY APPROPRIATELY

If you are submitting a paper-based application, don't underestimate the importance of your essay's physical appearance. Make sure that it is easy to read and that it makes a positive visual impression. Here are some specific points to keep in mind.

✎ IF THE SCHOOL PERMITS IT, PRESENT YOUR ESSAY ON A SEPARATE SHEET OF PAPER

However, resist any temptation to catch the reader's attention by using odd-sized paper, colored paper, letterhead, personalized stationery, or paper with preprinted pictures (e.g., smile faces) or phrases (e.g., "From the desk of . . ."). Use plain, white, high-quality, $8\frac{1}{2}'' \times 11''$ paper only, please.

✎ NUMBER EACH PAGE OF YOUR ESSAY, AND INCLUDE YOUR NAME AND SOCIAL SECURITY NUMBER ON EACH PAGE

This will ensure that your essays aren't lost or jumbled and will demonstrate your attention to detail.

✎ ASSEMBLE YOUR ESSAYS PROPERLY

Most schools indicate a particular order for you to assemble and present the various essays as well as other parts of your application. Be sure to comply with these guidelines or instructions. Use staples only if the school requests it.

✎ BE SURE TO COMPLY STRICTLY WITH ANY PAGE LIMITS THAT THE SCHOOL IMPOSES

Don't use small margins, line spacing, or fonts to squeeze a long essay onto a prescribed number of pages. Go back and shorten your essay instead. (Remember, brevity is a virtue in the eyes of admission officials.)

✎ DON'T WORRY TOO MUCH ABOUT THE SCHOOL'S WORD LIMITS

Nobody is going to count words or penalize you if you've exceeded the limit by a small margin. Try not to exceed the limit by more than ten percent, however. (This applies to electronic applications as well.)

✎ DON'T WRITE YOUR ESSAY IN LONGHAND

A handwritten essay would be justifiable, however, if either (1) the school requests it, (2) calligraphy is a serious hobby of yours, or (3) the subject of your essay in some way involves handwriting.

✎ USE HIGHLY READABLE FONTS

Fonts with serifs (stems at the tops and bottoms of the letters) are generally more readable than sans-serif fonts (fonts without the stems). Choose a readable point size (11–12 point). Don't use a gimmicky or fancy typeface. Finally, not all font software is comparable in quality. In a poor quality typeface, the "kerning" (spaces between letters) may be uneven, creating a sloppy visual impression.

✎ INCLUDE AMPLE MARGINS

Use 1″–1¼″ margins on all sides, unless the school specifies otherwise. That way your essay looks more appealing, and readers have space to write comments. Don't format your essay in columns.

✎ PRINT YOUR FINAL ESSAY ON A HIGH-RESOLUTION LASER PRINTER

Ink-jet print might smear or smudge. Use at least a 600 × 600 dpi (dots per inch) printer, if possible, for crisp, clean characters. Avoid colors—black text on white paper is best.

✎ DO NOT SUBMIT ESSAYS ON VIDEOTAPE OR AUDIOTAPE

If you have a terrific message but feel that you can convey that message effectively only through a medium other than print, check with the school first to see if they will allow it. Please don't refer the reader to your World Wide Web home page. It's *not* a novel idea, and admission personnel simply do not have the time for this.

✎ THINK TWICE BEFORE INCLUDING SUPPLEMENTARY MATERIALS

Unless the school encourages you to do so, do *not* submit to the admission office supplementary materials such as samples of your artwork, musical recordings or compositions, other writing samples, your science project, and the like. If you feel strongly that these materials would help your chances of admission, contact the school and ask whether you can send samples of your work to the appropriate academic department.

PART 2

50 Awesome Admission Essays

Okay, you now know a lot more about how to write an effective college admission essay. It would sure help, though, to see some essays that illustrate the advice in Part 1, wouldn't it? Look no further—they're right here!

All of the sample essays in Part 2 are authentic—written and submitted by successful applicants to real colleges. The essays here are quite diverse because the questions to which they respond are different and because each student brings his or her own style, personality, and "voice" to the essay. (Keep in mind as you read these samples, however, that some references to specific persons, schools, and other entities have been deleted.)

Don't even think about copying the sample essays in this book. They are intended to illustrate the advice and suggestions offered by admission officials as well as to inspire you and to spark ideas of your own; but they are *not* for copying. By plagiarizing a sample essay in this book, you will not only violate federal copyright laws but will also jeopardize your chances for admission to the college of your choice, since admission officials at many colleges will have read this book and will be on the lookout for essays that resemble the ones here.

A REVEALING LOOK AT THE REAL ME *(7 Essays)*

Essay No. 1

I can't tell you in which peer group I'd fit best because I'm a social chameleon and am comfortable in most; I will instead describe my own social situation and the various cliques I drift in and out of.

My high school's student body is from a part of town that is much more diverse than the rest of the city, and the city as a whole is more diverse than most of the state. The location of my school, only a few blocks from the University of Oregon, is greatly responsible for the social atmosphere. Whereas the other high schools in town draw mainly from middle-class white suburban families, mine sits in the division between the poor west university neighborhood and the affluent east university one. East university is hilly and forested with quiet residential streets and peaceful, large houses. A few blocks west, using the university as the divider, the houses become small and seedy. On the west side of my school there are many dirty apartments; crime is high and social status is low.

The result is the presence of two very distinct social scenes in the school itself. What is ironic although not crucial to this essay is that the school, a squat, gray-stained concrete sprawl, is divided right through the middle, just as its surrounding neighborhood is. The west wing ends in a gym, a symbol of lower-class recreation, and low aspiration, while the east wing holds the auditorium, the stronghold of sophistication, highbrow musical and theatrical achievement. On the east side are artsy wall murals, on the west side only graffiti.

The west parking lot holds mostly dirty pickup trucks, low-rider gangster cars and dilapidated, inherited little Hondas. The east lot is the home of numerous Mercedes and Chevy Suburbans, the gas-guzzlers and the late-models. The A.P. classes are strongly rooted in the east end; the remedial ones are clustered around the west athletic facilities. I burden you with this description in order to display the split, both social and geographic, that characterizes my academic life.

My classes are almost entirely on the east end of school; I'm attracted to them in a polar fashion as if I were a positively charged little scholastic particle, happily magnetized to the center of learning. However, despite the fact that I am fully integrated and comfortable in the intellectual east-end society, the stereotypical education robot is something I am not. My primary social scene is a contrast to the nerd-set.

Understand that I'm a snowboarder and that the Oregon snowboard culture is not some obscure athletic fringe group; on the contrary, it is quite defined, almost established in the mainstream. It is complete with its own dialect, style and customs. The rest of the snowboarders in school are undeniably members of the west halls and their houses are on the wrong side of the university.

I spend my lunches with my fellow nerds. We go to coffee shops and delis. I'm accepted as one of them. My larger-than-normal pants and similar statements of snow-style are recognized as superficial. However, I spend my weekends with the other crew. We go to parties and up to the mountain. We share the same discoloration of our faces, tan and leathery on the cheeks and forehead, pale around the eyes. Our faces bear the scars of wearing snowboarding goggles too often in the bright sun, and are proof of our membership in the snow posse, as indelible as the ornate tattoos that show gang alliances. Our tans demand respect from the kids in the west halls, for they are our social credentials in that end of the school, equivalent to standing on the varsity football team. Once associated with grungy skateboarders, the snowboard culture has found its own niche, just as surfing did before it. We now show much more similarity to jocks than to skater punks.

When I'm with my classmates, I'm one of them—a cultivated, upper-class young man. I'm invited to their houses and speak to their parents on a polite first name basis. When I hang out with boarders and jocks, I'm invited to their refuges and speak the rapidly shifting socialect. Very few of the students in my school drift socially as I do. As a result of the recent American infatuation with the alternative sub-culture, my classmates give me respect for embodying an unconventional trend while preserving my proper social standing. In the same sense, my clan from the wrong end of the school respects me for remaining faithful to our culture while succeeding academically; in their eyes I have found a way to get out of the social hole without selling out.

I'm perfectly comfortable with the fact that I don't have one single social identity. I think that if I only felt comfortable among kids from a certain end of the school, my life would be less interesting.

Essay No. 2

Last year, when the Duke football team beat Virginia and students carried the north goal-post to the main quad, I was one of many who scratched their names into the uprights. But there was one difference: I scratched "Stephen Byers, Class of 2000." For that one instant, I belonged to Duke, and Duke belonged to me.

Two-and-a-half years ago, I visited Duke for the first time with my older sister. I was the first to say, "This is where I want to go to college." Jenn was angry with her little brother for that remark because the trip was meant for her. That brief visit, and all others that followed, increased my determination to be accepted one day as a student at Duke. Having visited the campus many times over the past year, I have witnessed firsthand the academic challenge of the classroom experience as well as getting a taste of the university's social side. Since my first visit, I have met many Duke students who are genuinely excited about expanding their knowledge and about the challenging education that Duke provides.

Along with what Duke can offer me, I believe I have much to contribute to Duke. At the end of Easter mass in Page Auditorium last year, I discovered what community service means to students at Duke. As a graduating senior walked across the stage, she appeared composed and confident. After reaching the podium, she slowly described her role as a "big sister" to a young girl in Durham. Her voice began to crack. Composed again, she pleaded for someone to take over her responsibility to this girl. Even though the student was graduating within a month, she refused to leave Duke until someone agreed to take over her role. She was a young woman who really cared.

I have similar feelings for a brain-damaged girl with whom I work as a therapy volunteer. Petra has given me more than I could ever give her in return, and I will not stop giving what I can to others when I leave for college. I hope to encourage fellow classmates to get involved with service work in the Duke community because I know how rewarding volunteer work can be.

When I first realized I wanted to go to Duke, it was because my sister was looking at a top university. It was then that my dream to attend Duke began—a dream that I hope will soon become a reality.

Essay No. 3

There is something you should know about me right off the bat. It's not something I confess lightly, but here goes: I am an optimist. There, now that I've said it, I feel better. It's not as though I haven't tried to give it up; I have. But I keep going back to it like a duck to water. What's so bad about being an optimist?

I was born with a joyful nature. I reportedly smiled the entire time I was in the nursery, and for the next four years or so I slept twenty out of twenty-four hours every day. Life already was a dream come true for me, but when I finally regained consciousness I experienced what turned out to be my earliest memory. It was a conversation with my father about my confusion as to whether a glass was half-empty of half-full. My father, at first, figured it was the "half" concept which baffled me, but it turned out to be the "empty" part I didn't get. He officially declared me an optimist on the spot, and the label stuck.

The news got around fast. The kids in the neighborhood discovered my flaw when I played peewee soccer. Our team, the Green Slime, almost always lost, which tended to dilute the enthusiasm of the players. Except for me, that is. Even with the score 14 to 0 in the last minute of the last quarter, I would be running up and down the field yelling "Score, score, score!" resulting in my teammates' kicking the ball *at* me rather than to me. My grandmother discovered my optimism while we were watching a movie on television. In one scene, a car skidded through a guard rail, bounced off the side of a cliff, exploded into a ball of fire and plunged into the sea a hundred feet below. I turned to my grandmother and cheerfully said, "That wouldn't necessarily kill you, you know," prompting her to exchange meaningful glances with my mother, apparently questioning my judgment or sanity, or both.

Soon I was going to school where my former teammates had to put up with me as a classmate. My habit of waving my hand to answer any question and talking cheerfully about nearly every subject, no matter how catastrophic, did not endear me to them. My optimism even got to my teacher. She became fed up with my dismissal of her favorite topics— pollution, global warming and endangered species—as nothing to worry about. Unable to attack me directly, perhaps due to my good spelling and reading quiz scores, she took out her anger on my poor messy desk. In order to embarrass me, she made me empty everything out of my "cubby" and desk onto the floor and stand in front of the class. For the first time in my life, I was aware that perhaps not everyone thought well of me, and I became concerned and confused. After that, I kept my desk neat and clean, but my spirit was dampened. Had this sort of experience continued, I suppose I might have turned out like everyone else. But as luck would have it, my mother decided at this point to pull my sister and me out of class for home schooling.

In home schooling I was allowed the freedom to explore the world as I wished. I didn't have to read about whatever catastrophe people were currently bemoaning, and so I feasted on the Italian Renaissance, the novels of Victor Hugo, and the movies by Frank Capra, Billy Wilder, and Ernst Lubitsch. During these years of degenerate self-indulgence, my optimism flowered like algae in an aquarium.

I eventually dropped back into school because I decided that I should get a diploma since I wanted to go to college, and for a time my father actually held out hope that my optimism might be cured. The return to school, however, had little effect, for by that time I was a recognized and confirmed optimist with little hope of recovery.

Perhaps with time I will one day become cynical and mature, losing my naive, childish beliefs. But for the time being, I'll make a confession: I don't think I will. The truth is, I intend to keep on being an optimist. After all, here we are clinging to a tiny speck of dust called Earth, hurtling through space and going who knows where. And all we have is this little time squeezed between two great silences. So what is there to be pessimistic about?

Essay No. 4

When I was four years old I decided to challenge conventional notions of the human limit by flying through a glass window. The impetus was Superman, whose exploits on television had induced my experiment. Nine stitches and thirteen years later, while I no longer attempt to be stronger than steel or faster than a speeding bullet, I still find myself testing my limits, mental and physical.

It seems that I have spent my life getting into one thing or another. From that ill-fated flight to my recent trials and tribulations trying to repair my personal computer, I try to involve myself in as many things as I can. You could call me curious. Some people are apprehensive about being labeled "curious," associating the word with mischief and prying, but I think the word fits who I am. After all, "curious" is defined as "eager to acquire knowledge."

I'm eager. When I was in kindergarten my teacher told my father I was a hyperactive and unruly child. Claiming no kid of his was "hyperactive," my father promptly took me out of the school. To be honest, Dad wasn't completely right. I am a person who can never sit still. My sister calls me a time bomb when I drive because my hands are always fidgeting with the radio dials, the air conditioner, and other gadgets. When I want something, I can't wait. As an anxious eight year old, I remember driving my family nuts in anticipation of that staple of the 80's family, the Nintendo. I remember spending the night before pitching for my baseball team in the district playoffs polishing my cleats and organizing everything so it would be perfect. Now I spend sleepless nights dreaming about my future—what I'm going to do, where I'm going to be, and how I'm going to get there.

I am eager to acquire knowledge. For my ninth birthday, my father gave me a set of the *World Book Encyclopedia*. Although I would rather have received a set of transformers, as I look back I realize that my Dad made the right decision. While I have not read every volume of the encyclopedia from cover to cover, it is safe to say that when opened, the books don't close right back up again. As a kid I made it a practice to read a few pages every day before I went to sleep. The way I look at it, all that trivia is prepping me for Jeopardy!

You can call me curious. You can call me eager to acquire knowledge. You can call me Isaac.

Essay No. 5

Thinking. Plato did it, Freud studied it, Rodin sculpted it. Learning to do it critically can be difficult. Some never learn how, while for others it just comes naturally. I personally have "thought" the vast majority of my life. It was a talent I never considered. I just practiced. A friend once bought me a button that read, "I think, therefore I'm dangerous." He said it described me well. I suppose he was right.

I cultivated my thinking in seventh grade. I was in a gifted and talented program deep in Mandeville, Louisiana. We studied from books dug out of high-school dumpsters. Class was held in an old garage with makeshift classrooms that carried throughout the building the voice of each conjecture, the fire across each synapse. Some sixty of us studied there, bombarded by that barrage of thought. There was a real energy in that secondhand atmosphere, though. Our teachers did more than promote lofty erudite conversation; that makeshift environment encouraged real-life application of our lessons. We learned to read like thinkers, write like thinkers, experiment like thinkers. We evolved into real students.

Until I went to Mandeville, I considered my "giftedness" something rather unremarkable, even burdensome. All it seemed to bring me was extra homework in my Gifted-and-Talented class, boredom in the regular classroom, and estrangement from my peers. Junior high changed all of that. During my middle-school years I didn't learn about peer pressure, high hair or kissing. I learned how to balance chemical equations. I learned how to write eight-page term papers. I learned "mastication," "genre," and "tatterdemalion." Being an anomaly of the pre-teen world was legitimate there. I was gifted, and I was fine.

Mandeville's G/T program was truly extraordinary. Twenty-eight of us, from all walks of life, banded together there in a rather strange group. We didn't all get along, but a sense of respect infused our relationships and our classrooms. We were all spared labels like "nerd" and "brain." We bonded through a tremendous connection: the capabilities of our minds. A sense of family developed based on our similar learning experience. Having challenging material presented to us was an enthralling treat. I was so eager to consume and digest this newfound knowledge that I never stopped to doubt myself. I was too busy learning to doubt. I developed real confidence in my strengths as a student.

The support system we developed in those years made a substantial difference in how we handled our giftedness. When I started school at age four, my teachers hailed me as a genius, a prodigy with a photographic memory. Halfway through first grade, I was advanced another year. All the grand prognostications and expectations came crashing down. I did not have the memory. I could not handle the transfer. I was not a prodigy. I always felt I had disappointed these people in some way; I never wanted to let them down. My experience at Mandeville helped me to accept my disability as well as my ability. None of us were geniuses, but we all knew that we were still talented individuals. Intelligent, not brilliant. And that was okay.

I had to leave that school after two years. My mom decided it was time for her to return to school, a goal that could be obtained by moving back to the Great White North. We moved to Cloquet, Minnesota in 1988. Despite boasting the only Frank Lloyd Wright designed service station, Cloquet was no home to the higher world of academia. It was the home of a paper mill. I returned to a school world some might call reality; I was a "brain" and a "geek" again. Lucky for me that I had already learned the value of my mind. Although I've done more than my share of self-doubting, I know that I am a thinker. I know what I love to learn, and that in this, I am not alone.

Essay No. 6

The sky was mottled with clumps of white. I stood on the border between the track and the field, my eyes intently fixed on one particular clump. As the wind rustled by, the white began to fade from view. I remained fixated. The cloud became wisps, and the wisps, in turn, became smaller and bluer until there was no white remaining. I blinked and turned away.

My Theory of Knowledge teacher, Mr. Coleman, defines cloud-poofing as the willful dissipation of a small cloud. The process is simple: one selects the cloud for extinction, concentrates on the chosen cloud, and wills it to dissipate. Intending to master the art of cloud poofing, my class marched outside on a windy April afternoon. Along with the others, I planted myself in one spot and stared up at the sky. After everyone had poofed at least one cloud, we reentered the building, and, as part of our discussion, divided into two factions: the believers and the non-believers. Everyone, that is, except for me.

The skeptic, a logician, would say that the weather that day was no accident, that had we ventured outside on a windless day, the experiment would have failed. He would attribute the clouds' sudden disappearance to gusts of wind. All clouds, he would continue, form and then dissipate. We were an irrelevance. The "creatician," in contrast, would claim that the skeptic has been influenced by societal conventions. Less affected by science and logic, the creatician would see no reason why the mind could not affect the clouds, and know that the skeptic cannot, no matter how hard he tries, prove otherwise.

I am the logician. I am the creatician. In that classroom, surrounded by the noise of fervent discussion, I felt the resurgence of a conflict I had come to know well. The two sides of my personality had begun to vie for intellectual supremacy. Part of my mind, the logical side, agreed with the logician in saying that not only is the simplest explanation the best one but also that the mind has no power to alter external stimuli.

"Logic," preaches the logician. "Remember and heed logic."

"Wait!" retorts the science disregarder, the creatician. "You, logician, have no proof that the mind is confined to the internal world. You just assume it because science and logic tell you so."

As always, neither side is able to convince the other. The war continues to wage itself, and I live as a tumultuous battleground.

The unresolved conflict between my logical and creative sides pervades everything I do, believe, and am. I love the poetic and descriptive power of words. I enjoy nothing more than flurries of figurativeness. Playing with the power of these words and altering them is one of my specialties. Still, I am often the strict grammarian, who organizes his prepositions and distinguishes between the dash and the colon. He is not concerned with flow or flower, only syntax and punctuation. In physics, I am the scientist; momentum is mass times velocity and everything is composed of atoms. In a field, gazing at the sun as it descends through the trees, I feel, I know that I am not the components of a rock rearranged. Beethoven, I am aware, composed impeccably, and for his perfection I salute him. Mozart, however, despite his theoretical shortcomings, affects me more deeply and sincerely. I can criticize his composition, but I can never suppress the intense feeling his music stirs within me.

The result of being pulled in both directions is that I am characterized by a certain chaos. Far from harming me, my chaotic nature is the source of my individuality. Somehow, my conflicting sides benefit each other even as they battle each other. The logician within me ensures that my writing is clear and grammatically correct; the creatician adds flavor and originality. Without logic, I could not use science and the conventions of philosophy, and without merging logic with creativity, I would be unable to develop my own uniquely chaotic deviations. I am chaos incarnate, but the chaos works.

Essay No. 7

[Attached to the following essay was a piece of paper with the following handwritten words: "Great organization. You rock and sway to the point of making your audience seasick."]

I still wonder why I kept this debate judge's ballot from the first time I competed in expository speaking. It's not as if those comments bring back fond memories of overwhelming success. Apparently, the hand gestures I so desperately tried to include, combined with a constant shifting back and forth on my feet, produced an effect quite different from the one I had intended to achieve. I didn't even belong up there, anyway. An experienced debater, well-versed in the art of speaking on the spur of the moment, I had crossed over into the realm of rehearsed speech, a place which *"true"* debaters classified as infinitely inferior. Yet despite this, I still cannot deny it: speech and debate together constitute the activity that is most meaningful for what they have shown me about myself.

When I first started debating, it was as if I had found a different person inside of me. Like Dr. Jekyll and Mr. Hyde, I would transform from a normally quiet and reserved young man into a frenzied speaker whose words came out so fast they bordered on unintelligible. The pressure of each round stripped away my inhibitions, leaving nothing standing between me and victory. After a year of experiencing the thrill of arguing against fellow debaters, I entered expository speaking to occupy the time in-between debate rounds. As I soon discovered, "Mr. Hyde" would not work for speech competitions since the speed and argumentation of debate are not compatible with the composure and presentation needed for speech. Despite some initial setbacks, I continued participating and in turn, soon realized that I could be calm and rational while speaking at length on a chosen topic instead of tense and critical or shy and tentative.

Strange as it may seem, I sometimes think that I must have multiple personalities or else I would never get through a debate tournament. From nervously waiting for a round to begin to urgently appealing a judge to consider my arguments to projecting confidence and authority during a speech, public speaking has brought out many different sides of me. While these vast extremes may lead one to think that I need immediate psychological help, I remain grateful for learning that I am not confined to be only "one" person. And perhaps that is why I did not throw away that ballot in disgust. It represents the surfacing of yet another aspect of my personality, one I am proud of . . . even if it does make people seasick.

MEANINGFUL METAPHORS AND SYMBOLIC KEEPSAKES *(6 Essays)*

Essay No. 8

When I was in the eighth grade, my backpack disappeared from my life. I can't remember what happened to it. I may have lost it, or perhaps my sister took it. Anyway, I found myself backpackless. I need a backpack to carry all my books, binders, pens, pencils, highlighters, protractors, calculators and compasses (sometimes I go a bit overboard with the tools I bring to class). I began to use this strange pack of my dad's, which was actually more like a soft-sided briefcase with back-straps. That pack was truly the ugliest piece of luggage I have ever seen. It embarrassed my friends and made me feel like a fool, but I had no choice but to wear it. I couldn't find any alternative where I lived in Saudi Arabia, so I promptly ordered a backpack from L.L. Bean.

I really enjoy pouring over catalogs, so I enthusiastically decided on the nine-inch deep L.L. Bean Deluxe (I need a roomy backpack). For the color, I debated among eggplant, forest green, pine, and the other excitedly-named shades, but eventually decided on mallard blue. It was a shade of blue that bordered on iridescent. I knew no one else would have a backpack that color. I sent off my order form and eagerly waited.

It takes a few months for L.L. Bean to get something all the way to Saudi Arabia, but my backpack eventually arrived. I realized that mallard blue had been a bold choice. The color could definitely be called ugly, and its brightness could not be denied. It was also huge, especially on my eighth-grade body. The crowning detail was my initials "H-A-W" embroidered on the back. Yes, it spells "haw." However, it was clearly an improvement over Dad's dork-case. I loved it, and it has since gone with me everywhere.

My bag has acquired a great deal of character since eighth grade. There are little marks and scratches all over the material. There's a small sparkly bead flower I sewed on once in a fit of procrastination; the flower was originally accompanied by a diagonal line of sparkly beads above the reflective strip on the bag, but I decided that was just too much and removed the line of beads. One can faintly see where I wrote "excess" on the bag. I don't know why I wrote that; I just went through a phase when I thought "excess" was a cool word. Also on the bag is leftover stitching from where I had attached a Saudi Arabian flag, which I removed because I feared it made me vulnerable to terrorist attacks. On the back pocket, I added a patch proclaiming me to be an "advanced" diver from the scuba class I took during the summer. When I have time, I plan to add another patch from NOLS, the National Outdoor Leadership School, where I spent part of my summer. The final touch is a little guardian angel pin that my aunt gave to me. It looks silly in its shiny golden newness next to the rest of my rugged ragged bag, but I could think of no better place for the pin, which I'm supposed to keep near me at all times.

I think my backpack is a good representation of me. Just like my backpack, my personality is full of random, loud elements that don't really make sense together. Their only unifying force is the fact that they all belong to me, so I like them. Just as my backpack has picked up a patch here and a beaded design there, I have picked up ideas here and insights there throughout our travels together. It records my history more personally than a diary ever could, and although I know it is just a material object, I would be at a loss if I were ever to lose it.

Essay No. 9

Spaceships, fireboats, castles, trucks, and pirate ships are just a handful of the countless projects I have constructed throughout my childhood. No, I was not some child prodigy enveloped in the world of construction. I just had an undying passion for a tiny piece of molded plastic. I went through many toy phases as I progressed from pre-kindergarten through eighth grade, but the toys that I have always come back to are the ones that can become something different every time I use them: the Lego building blocks.

My original exposure to the world of Lego was at the age of five. I remember fondly the younger brother of the Lego, the Duplo. Duplo blocks were generally much larger and simpler than Lego blocks. An entire car could be made from five or six Duplo blocks. After graduating out of Duplos, I entered the amazing world of Legos. From that point on I accumulated quite a collection of Legos, enough to fill four massive crates.

My pride and joy was a lunar base I designed that covered nearly four square feet of my room. I played with it constantly and I continued to add to it until one dark day when my good friend Andy fell on the base during a vicious pillow fight, completely destroying the whole thing. Andy and I are still good friends, but I will never forgive him for demolishing my prized possession.

Legos have had an immeasurable effect on my life. They shaped my childhood, and as a result, they have also shaped me into the person I am today. My development is strangely parallel to that of the development of any Lego project. Every Lego project begins with an assortment of pieces, all different shapes and colors. Some pieces I find to be essential to the project, while others can be discarded. I always start with a basic foundation. From that point, I build up and out until it is no longer a set of random blocks. It has taken shape and has become something that now has its own identity. My life began with exposure to a variety of experiences, and throughout my childhood, I learned to develop my values based on all these different experiences. Eventually, a form began to emerge that distinguished me from everyone else.

Legos may not have changed the world the way the airplane and the computer have, but for one little boy, they accomplished what no incredible piece of technology could do. They released an unstoppable flow of imagination and curiosity that has shaped the boy into a creative, energetic, and confident young man.

Essay No. 10

If each person's life could be likened to a book, the early chapters of mine would be some of the fullest. For more than six years, I was a partaker of the pageantry of European history and culture. My childhood in Munich, Germany, and my travels throughout the continent have shaped me in countless ways. I want to share with you one small chapter of my life which took place in Florence, Italy, where I became acquainted with a man named David.

His sheer immensity is what I remember most, a mute giant whose face said a thousand words, a marble god brought forth by the worshipping artist. From above, a gray-blue nimbus flowed from the skylight, not reflecting or refracting but rather rippling and gliding, becoming part of his silken mane and sinewy limbs.

I reached out my child's hand, plump with life, and brushed his ashen toe. There was a violent collision of the real and the fantastic, the breathing human being and the living art. I raised my eyes to his, and mine were locked in their embrace, knowing that they would never turn away. I set my palm flat against his pedestal, I was entranced by the cool warmth of the stone. David, with your fleeting frown and casual pose . . . how did you have the courage to fight mighty Goliath? Ah, but how could a seven-year-old girl see him thus, you say. It is the seventeen-year-old who now knows what I saw that day—human potential in its purest form.

Michelangelo captured not a moment but a lifetime. Never have I stood or will I stand again in such awe of life itself. Glancing back, alone, in the softly falling dust motes, I knew. I knew the greatness of man, and I am filled with its marble weight even now.

Essay No. 11

I hate contact paper. You know, the paper with flowery designs on one side and impossibly sticky glue on the other; the kind that pastes to the shelves in the cabinets. You'd understand my dislike—no, extreme hatred—if you've ever had to paper thirty-five shelves, twenty-eight drawers, ten boxes, and a partridge in a pear tree. Not only is it four days of back-breaking work, it is pure torture trying to make the paper cooperate. Perhaps a quick lesson on how I paper shelves would be enlightening:

(1) First, I figure out the amount of contact paper I need. Although the paper manufacturer thoughtfully placed measured intervals on the back of the paper, the carpenter "conveniently" created the shelves somewhat unevenly, measuring sixteen-point-two inches by twenty-point-three inches. Of course, now those nifty lines on the back of the contact paper have no use due to the "artistic liberty" of a carpenter who would not recognize a ruler if shown one. So what am I to do? Thinking rationally, I derive a simple equation to compute the exact quantity required. All I need to know is, oh, basic calculus.

(2) Next, I separate the paper from the backing. This is where I undergo vigorous exercise. The enterprise that produces this paper leaves a minuscule half-millimeter of space in which to jam my fingernail, in my torturous effort to separate them. However, I have found that by holding the paper between my legs, with one hand firmly gasping the

actual contact paper, the other hand grabbing the backing, and by jumping up and down (in the same manner as squeezing into jeans after the holiday season), I should be able to finish that process in, oh say, ten minutes. (My record is nine minutes and forty-four seconds.)

(3) Now that the papers are finally separated, I reluctantly perform the most tedious part. This part appears to be relatively simple: I put the paper, sticky side down, on the shelf. Unfortunately, life is just not that considerate. This paper has crazy glue on the back. If it gets caught on a table top, to itself, to the door, to your hair, or to your brother, it's going to stay there. Trust me (my brother wouldn't speak to me for a week since the paper is waterproof). As for the paper on the shelf, I need to put it down exactly where I want it to be; a slight miscalculation of the eye creates a wrinkle that is permanent.

So much for enlightenment. What's my point? Well, contact paper is similar to my way of relating to people (ah-hah!). Note the similarities:

(1) First, like figuring out the amount of contact paper, I have to find the group of people I am most like. Usually, everyone is kind enough to present me with a brief overview of his or her life (a.k.a., facade) that seems perfect and evenly made. I, however, do not fit in with these "flawless" people. I have that extra three-quarter inches on my hips . . . and in my personality. I'm a little offbeat and a bit eccentric; belonging to the "norm" is calculus to me.

(2) Trying to get to know people away from the cliques that formed in middle school is vigorous exercise. These people are attached like glue to their childhood ideas, and they refuse to let go of their prehistoric rituals. In my adolescent effort to gain acceptance, I undergo various physical transformations. Hence, the squeezing myself into the too-tight jeans.

(3) Even though I think I have finally found that circle of friends, I often come upon the discovery that I have a million

other obstacles to hurdle. And in the case of humans, one mistake might become an everlasting wrinkle in our relationship.

Looking back, the search for my niche has not been that horrible. Even though I have not been able to find the precise clique in which to belong, I have met a variety of people. This diversity of personalities has helped broaden my horizons and experiences. Though there have been difficult times, the end result of a cultured and multifaceted background has been well worth the obstacles. After all, it's the social bumps and bruises that create a distinct, mature character; social pressures have humanized me much the same way geological pressure turns coal into diamonds.

So it's not surprising that I have discovered that contact paper isn't that bad—when used for the right purpose. In a recent meeting of the March of Dimes Chain Reaction Youth Council, we made grief boxes. Grief boxes are for mothers whose babies are stillborn or die during birth. The council makes the boxes and the hospital puts in the baby's birth certificate, death certificate, and a baby blanket. We made the grief parcels by taking regular shoe boxes and covering the box and lid with pretty contact paper. Then we glued white flannel around the inside, and added lace around the top with a ribbon bow. Very touching and thoughtful. For once, I was not upset about all the tedious work created by the contact paper. I was really glad that I would be able to make a grieving mother's day a little brighter. Maybe I don't hate contact paper. Maybe I just thought I did.

Essay No. 12

I own a diamond so small that you have to look closely to distinguish it from its base. Surrounding the mineral is a thin line of gold forming the shape of a Jewish star. A gold chain holds the star and when you place it around your neck, you have to be careful that the diamond side faces forward.

I was fourteen years old when I found it wrapped up in tissue paper, awaiting my return from the synagogue. A small piece of paper had been ripped and folded to make a card which read: "Congratulations on your Bat-Mitzvah. Love, Dad." That is all my father had to say. He drove up from his Christian home to enter my Jewish world, leaving his new family of three to join his old family of four. He watched as I was accepted into the world of Jewish adults. I valued the necklace only because it was the first time in seven years my dad and mom came together without screaming or causing tears. Thus, it becomes a charm of good luck.

The necklace stayed clasped around my neck twenty-four hours a day and eventually traveled with me to Israel. I held it in my hands for a sense of protection as I flew out of San Francisco and held it once again as I landed on foreign ground. For six weeks, my thoughts kept returning to home and to the security of not worrying about daily acts of violence between two peoples fighting for one piece of land. When I mistakenly entered the Arab side of the Wailing Wall, it seemed as though my necklace grew large and those who looked in my direction saw only the small star that hung from my neck. My hand reached to hold it as I quickly left their place of reverence, squeezing the star so that it made indentations on my fingers. I only pressed harder until my feet led me back to the Jewish side of the white stones that make up the Wailing Wall. My necklace brought me strength and the harder I pressed my fingers against it, the more secure I felt.

While the shape of my star stayed the same, the shape of my life took off in many directions. I still wore my necklace, but always over my required uniform of the Papa Murphy's Pizza shirt and apron. Tomato paste and oil splattered onto the chain and occasionally onto the stone. One evening, an irritable old man came in near closing. As I took his order, I noticed that he too wore a Star of David. I started a conversation meant to last seconds that turned into ten minutes. We talked of voyages to Israel, Rabbis that made us question, and my distaste for parsley and salt at Passover Seders. I left work that night and walked in the cold air caressing my star with a sense of connection, a feeling of closeness to the people of my faith.

I cautiously placed my necklace around my neck as I once again boarded a plane to leave for Jonquiere, Quebec. For the following six weeks, I studied in a country where few people knew of the Jewish religion, and where those who looked at my necklace noticed it only for its beauty. Classmates in my courses knew of Judaism solely through stereotypes from television. For many, I was the first Jew they had met. I spoke less of my faith as a Jew, yet noticed its impact on me more. My necklace was my identity. I pulled it from underneath my shirt and placed it on the outside of my clothing, not caring if the diamond side faced forward.

Essay No. 13

"Have you ever noticed that the people never rip the paper off their gifts? The boxes are rigged so that the lid will simply lift off." Some time after sharing this insight with my friend Jennifer, I received a birthday present from her wrapped in such a way that the top came off without tearing the blue paper. I kept the special box and placed my birthday cards in it along with a few other letters I regarded as treasures. Since then, I've moved across the country twice, but the box remains on the top shelf of my closet, now joined by two other shoe boxes, a pink, heart-shaped container, and a hand-woven Guatemalan bag—all overflowing with the letters that chronicle so much of my life and so many of my friendships.

My inability to part with any of my letters—from the shortest note from Grandma to one of the hundreds of letters from my friend Melissa—cannot be easily explained. Certainly the love letters play upon my conceit, gently building my fragile teenage self-esteem. Beyond these, however, lie the babbling prose of girlfriends, the one note I received from my camp roommate, and the letter accompanying the black and white photo of John, Paul, George, and Ringo which I won in the "Eight Days a Week" Beatles sweepstakes. I treasure each of these and hold tight the history locked within them in my changing world; to quote the opening of one of Melissa's letters, "Life is so wonderful, and so unfair, and so confusing."

Throughout my life, I have clung to any concrete portion of the world I could get my hands on, and I have developed a deep trust in, and yearning for, the written word. Unlike spoken words, written words have a timelessness; they hold a promise forever, and they bind the writer to his promise indelibly. Smashed between a slumber party invitation and a post card from Florida, my great grandmother will always be waiting "with love" inside a card decorated with lavender flowers. When someday I get married, my first boyfriend will still miss my "soft voice and soft eyes." I rarely need to check these reminders that I can never stop being loved, being a friend, and making a difference in the lives of others. I am always conscious of the gathering that awaits me in the dusty boxes. Each time I receive a new letter, I carefully place it into the little life museum perched on my closet shelf.

FAMILY TIES *(5 Essays)*

Essay No. 14

I did not appreciate her nightly ritual until I had grown taller than she. And it was even longer before I remembered that my first memories of her included the familiar sounds and smells which escaped from her kitchen each night. As she labors, her husband reads the day's Chinese newspaper, while down the hall her American daughter studies. Tonight, however, things are changing. Tonight her daughter is not so American.

I sit with my mother at the dining table and learn to make sushi for the first time. Not the Japanese kind with raw fish, but my mother's own creation. I first add rice vinegar and sugar to the just-cooked rice, mixing with the rice paddle. Spreading the rice on lightly-toasted nori, I pile on shreds of dried pork. On impulse, I decide to add in some octopus. When at last I am ready to roll the sushi, my mother is twinkling with soundless laughter, for my fingers, and even my shirt, are spotted with grains of sticky white rice.

I must hold the sushi firmly, then press down and roll; soon I find my own rhythm. My sushi-making surprises my parents, since they see me only as the daughter who refused to attend a second year of Chinese school, the child who no longer speaks Mandarin or Taiwanese.

Tonight I extend my arms across the ocean that separates my parents from me. I try to make up for the silent dinners and the stereotypes we cast on each other. My parents do not hear my words, just as I am sometimes deaf to theirs. They buy McDonald's for me, though I hate fast food. Even tonight—this attempt to get closer to my mother—is viewed as an aberration; they do not understand why I would care to make sushi. I fear that this attempt, and every one after tonight, will ultimately fail. I am, every day, moving away from my parents, and I walk these streets that are foreign to them but home to me. I cannot mend the ropes which tore with my first word of

English, the ropes which had begun to strain years ago at my first step. Though my parents may try, they do not define me. I am my own creator.

Still, I will try again another day, with impossible hopes that we can make a lasting connection. Now, for a little while, I listen to my mother tell me her childhood stories, and I unfold parts of myself.

These few hundred words are only a sliver of the entire me; you have tasted only a sprinkling of the ingredients in my sushi. If you wait, you will taste not only my cold cucumbers and my octopus, but also my words and thoughts swimming around your taste buds.

Essay No. 15

"He looks like Old Man Winter," my friend Mark said, looking at a picture of my grandfather, whose steel-white mustache and thinning wisps around his mostly bald scalp gave off a sense of warm wisdom and beneficence. In the picture he is holding my two-year-old cousin and because of that he smiles in happiness. "Is he the one who takes you skiing?"

"Yeah," I answered, "he taught me how to ski."

"Wow, cool guy."

Stubborn, sometimes miserly but often grandly generous, my grandfather has been one of the greatest positive influences in my life, and he is one of my few heroes. Though he did not always get along with his three daughters, he is definitely one of the greats in the eyes of his five grandchildren.

When I was two he bought a ski house in New Hampshire in order to teach his grandchildren to ski, having learned himself only five years earlier. At age five I was taken out to the mountain and, under my grandfather's instruction, was soon the terror of the bunny slope.

When I was eight, he put me on the tennis court with an oversized wooden racket in my hands, and proceeded to teach me the basics of the game, a game that he had himself learned only in his fifties. Over the past few summers, as I taught tennis at the camp at my school, I found his words coming out through my lips: "Keep your racket back, your eyes on the ball, and follow through." It has taken me this long to realize how much my grandfather has taught me. At eight years old it seemed natural to me that every time I went to my grandparents' house, he would take me to the Boston Science Museum and explain the latest exhibit. On the swan boats in the Public Gardens he would tell stories of the dangerous hospital ship he served on in World War II. I looked forward to long trips with him to Beth Israel Hospital for treatment of his psoriasis, even though when we got to the hospital I would have to sit in the car, looking out for the meter maid with a handful of change.

My grandfather was as well known for taking all his grandchildren out for tennis and a movie as he was for bringing the salesman at the Toyota dealership to the verge of tears, trying to cut a deal. He is as happy playing his violin as he is sitting down with a big bowl of chocolate ice cream. He taught me, above all else, that if there is something you want to do, there is a way to do it. His life is that story. Even though now, at 78, because of a bad knee he might not be able to play tennis or take me skiing as much as he'd like, he still sets the example for his grandchildren and teaches the lesson and that he has all along: never stop learning.

Essay No. 16

I keep remembering odd things: the way she loved daffodils, her delight at the antics of our dog, jokes she told at the dinner table, her subtle brand of feminism, the look in her eyes when she talked about my future. I knew about college before I'd ever heard of high school; I was Mom's second chance at the degree she never had.

Her parents pushed her too much, too hard, too fast, and she always wished she hadn't let the pressure overwhelm her. She dropped out of college after one semester for marriage and a secretarial job. While she never regretted marrying my father, she always regretted giving up her dream of becoming an accountant. She was determined her eldest daughter would never miss an opportunity, and she missed out on so many herself so I could succeed.

She was the one person I could talk to about anything: politics, dating, parties, failed tests, or nail polish. She was right about so much, so often—much more than I gave her credit for at the time. We never did agree on clothes. She favored the J. Crew look, I kept trying for (and failing at) the neo-sixties style. One year we didn't buy any new clothes at all in a battle of wills: she refused to buy anything that didn't "fit me properly" and I refused to wear anything with an alligator on it.

She loved the holidays, Christmas most of all. One of the most intensely special times of my life was Christmas my sophomore year, when I played Tiny Tim in a local community theater production of "A Christmas Carol." Mom delighted in my endless rehearsal stories and spent hours helping me work out ways of disguising my long hair. There's a line in the show: "And it was always said of him that he knew how to keep Christmas well, if any man alive possessed the knowledge." Change the pronouns and that quote describes Mom perfectly.

I never imagined she wouldn't be here now, micromanaging, debating the merits of such-and-such college with me, chasing the dog around the living room, ruining spaghetti, explaining "power colors," and relishing exciting changes in IRS forms. I never thought cancer could strike so quickly, could kill someone so strong and determined in only a year.

She's the one person I couldn't imagine living without; now, since last January, I've had to. Suddenly, I have no one to talk to about meaningless little things, no one whose advice I trust implicitly to help me with decisions. When I come home from school, I come home to an empty house, haunted by memories of the year she spent here dying. I remember the disastrous Thanksgiving when she was nauseous and delusional, our wonderful last Christmas Eve together, the tangle of tubes in the family room, the needlepoint picture of Rainbow Row she labored over while stuck in bed, and the bags of M&Ms she always kept within reach.

What I feel cheated of is the future we'll never have.

Essay No. 17

He was the best of brothers; he was the worst of brothers. Unfortunately, he was the worst—for a long time before I thought otherwise. In short, Mike did not fit my image of the ideal older brother. He was not a friend. Instead, he was my enemy, my nightmare, a bully from whom I could not escape. Just the thought of our horrible childhood encounters makes me cringe.

I can recall the nightly "pounding sessions" that left me screaming for my parents, and my parents screaming at Mike. In fact, it seemed as though they were always focused on my brother, usually for something he had done wrong. My friends' older brothers were their mentors, their protectors, their idols. Not mine. The only interaction we had consisted of physical and verbal abuse. Needless to say, there was not much affection between us.

I can't remember exactly when I discovered I was smarter than my brother, but it was early on and it afforded me the chance to gain at least the intellectual edge. I took great delight in bringing home better grades, beating him at family games, and winning our verbal encounters. I usually paid the price, but at least my pride stayed somewhat intact.

Two winters ago, my family took a ski vacation to Colorado. Many of our school friends were there, as well. We skied, we ate, we partied. I tried to avoid Mike as best I could, but when we were together, he never missed an opportunity to torment me, especially in front of the others.

One particularly frigid morning found my brother, a mutual friend, and me perched tentatively (at least I was) atop a narrow, plunging slope. Trees lined both sides, and the sun had yet to make any impact on the ice-encrusted snow. Mike went first. He made two turns, lost his balance, and began to career downhill, clearly out of control. Our eyes widened as we saw him veer left and disappear into the forest. "Mike!" we screamed several times. There was no sound.

I could feel a churning sensation in my stomach as we quickly made our way down to the spot where we had last seen my brother. The forest was dense and dark, and it swallowed our frantic cries without reply. I had already kicked off my skis and begun to tread through deep snow in the direction of Mike's tracks when I saw him. He lay motionless between two trees, and I was sure he was dead.

"Get a doctor!" I pleaded with our friend. As he skied away, I approached my brother, terrified. "Mike," I repeated several times as I stared at the bloody scrape above his left eye. He did not respond, but I was almost sure he was breathing. I knew not to move him, and the only thing I could think to do was keep him warm until help arrived. I lay at his side and tried to cover as much of him with my body as possible without any weight.

That's when my mind began to race. I had wished him dead so many times and now that it seemed a distinct possibility, somehow I felt responsible. I was actually afraid that it might happen, and feelings began to surface that had been lost or repressed for as long as I could remember. My whole body heaved and shook. As I found myself praying for

Mike's life, I began to question my role in our relationship. In my mind I had always been the "victim," the innocent object of his wrath. I had never accepted any responsibility for our lack of closeness, but suddenly I realized that I had played a major part as well. I was a master at infuriating Mike; I knew the right "buttons to push" and enjoyed seeing him and my parents fight. I delighted in the frustration Mike felt when I brought home scholastic awards and straight A's. My brother was the perfect foil; and in some twisted way I actually owed him a great deal, for he was the inspiration for much of my motivation and success, a reverse role model.

Suddenly I didn't seem so innocent, I had used Mike as he had used me, and our relationship was the real victim. I truly felt compassion for him and wondered if this new and strange sensation was "brotherly love." As it turned out, Mike had a concussion, no broken bones, and had to sit out the rest of our vacation in bed. I finished the week a slightly better skier and a brother who had found a new level of understanding about accepting responsibility, and one who had rediscovered some long-forgotten emotions.

A year and a half later I am happy to report that our relationship is much improved. We still don't have a great deal in common, but we do have a newfound respect for each another; and although we still bicker and fight, I sense a growing connection between us. Mike called home from college last week and asked to speak with me. We actually had a meaningful conversation, and it felt wonderful.

Essay No. 18

All eyes were focused on me. This was it. The tension had been building up to this point, and I knew there was no way out. I had gotten myself into this predicament, and I was the only one that could get myself out of it. There was nobody to turn to, for they were all waiting for my final move. I had never felt so alone, so isolated.

I thumbed through my cards for the fourth consecutive time, and I could still not decide which one to throw. I glanced up from my cards and caught a glimpse of each player. I immediately felt the intensity of my brother's eyes glaring at me from across the table. He did not provide me with the support and reassurance I was looking for from my partner. I shifted my eyes to the right. My mother, having just discarded a five of clubs and seeing that it was of no use to me, was sipping coffee with a carefree grin of relief. Then I peered directly at the most intimidating canasta player I have ever encountered. Great Grandma Rose was calmly humming a tuneless tune which added to her enigma. As this crafty eighty-eight year old lady squinted at her cards through her bifocals, I knew that time was running out; I had to make my decision. The most obvious choice was to discard the king of spades for which I had no use, but I was afraid that she was waiting for this card. My alternative was to break up my meld and throw the six of clubs, a card which I felt somewhat safe in throwing.

In the midst of my despair, great grandma delivered the final blow. She stopped humming and uttered these dreaded words: "It only hurts for a minute."

She could not have dug a knife any deeper. My brother's eyes were flaring with tension, I had complete control over his fate, and I knew our team unity was riding on the outcome of my decision. I therefore decided to play defensively and throw the six of clubs. No sooner had my discard settled on top of the pile than my great grandmother's hand darted out to snatch up the stack of cards and my brother simultaneously belted out a scream. "The six of clubs? How could you throw the six of clubs!"

I wanted to ask him if the king of spades would have been any better, but I knew a rebuttal was useless. I knew he would get over it soon enough, and like Grandma Rose says, "It only hurts for minute!"

After my great grandma laid down her meld and sorted her cards, the game continued (and so did her humming). Although we lost that particular hand, my brother and I miraculously came back to snatch victory from the jaws of defeat. As we reveled in our triumph (my brother had now forgiven me for discarding the six of clubs), I could not resist directing my newly acquired quote at our opponents, who were mulling over their defeat. "Well, I have only one thing to say." My smile was so big that I could feel my cheeks stretching. "It only hurts for a minute."

Although my great grandmother had no intention of being profound, this quote actually embodies an important concept. Many people spend so much time worrying about the infinite possibilities that may result from any decision they make that they actually never make a decision at all. Although it is necessary to weigh the options and consider various viewpoints, excessive deliberation can often be detrimental. From personal experience, I have found it is usually better to think about the choices and come to a firm decision rather than to prolong the problem and perhaps create a new one by avoiding a commitment one way or the other. The best course of action is to make the wisest choice possible with the available information and then to make the most out of your initial decision. Even if in retrospect you see a better alternative, you can always pursue a new direction based on what you have learned through this experience. Surprisingly, what may at first appear to be failure may often spark an unforeseen success. I have learned not to let undue hesitation hinder my ability to take advantage of opportunities. After all, as my great grandmother so eloquently remarked during those heated canasta games, "It only hurts for a minute!"

TERRIFIC TEACHERS *(4 Essays)*

Essay No. 19

"Breez in and breez out. Clear yor mind by zinking of somezing plasant." For five minutes, all of us found ourselves sitting cross-legged on the floor with a soft, sleepy look on our faces as we subconsciously nodded to the soothing rhythmic voice of our French teacher. Our heads were still half wafting in the delicious swirls of dreamland, barely dwelling in the bittersweet shock of reality. Time whizzed by swiftly and we were forced to tend to the grueling task of untangling our aching frames, stiffened from prolonged straining positions.

Madame DuPont would then launch into her lesson plan for the day with much animation. She often exuded boundless vitality and seemed to bounce with every step she took, while the rest of us were just starting to recover from the morning blues. I imagined her to be another Napoleon Bonaparte, seeking to instill in us a certain form of discipline as she led us in the formidable mission of conquering the French language.

As we tried hopelessly to mimic her genuine Parisian accent, she would persistently encourage us by dictating, "Errrroll yor Rrrrr's *messieurs* et *mesdemoiselles*! You must enunciate yor vowels and consonants properly! . . . *Oui*, zat's it!" Whenever we succeeded in our strenuous efforts, she would reward us with her trademark impish grin. The sight of her lively expression often led our hearts to be consoled with instant relief and a true sense of achievement. Her optimistic attitude toward life itself proved to be highly contagious, for it made us even more susceptible to learning. Our steadfast attentions never failed to drift away to the soporific world of daydreams, designated in our minds as No Man's Land. The mystic ambiance she generated from her manner and her unique style of teaching was somehow bewitching. Whether she was instructing us in the conjugation of *savoir* or assisting us in differentiating between the usage of *avoir* and *être* in relation to other verbs, she always did it *avec beaucoup de plaisir*. She was a special individual who would help others without request and who was willing to listen to people's problems without prejudice. In her I found a role model as well as a friend who I could depend on.

She firmly believed the path to successful learning was to make sure the materials presented were enlightening yet intriguing and never too tedious. I was always amazed at how she was able to arouse in us such an enduring interest in French. This enigma perplexed me, and I vowed to unveil her secret one day. I did not get the opportunity to discover her formula for success, for she moved away soon after I made the pledge to myself. However, not long after her departure I received an unexpected letter from her that satisfied my lingering curiosity. Within its content, I realized what I had been searching for had been there since the very first day I walked into her class. It was the self-confidence she possessed and the staunch belief that she could make a difference that made her a lasting success in my mind.

Essay No. 20

If the lesson of life is happiness, then I have met the most dramatic of teachers. By the world's standards, my "teacher's" words are far from eloquent, his style far from graceful, his works far from wondrous. Yet in his determination and courage I see a hero, a hero unlike those we normally choose. He is Patrick, and, by the way, he has Down Syndrome.

Working as the dance and movement specialist during the summer of 1994 at Carousel Farm, a summer camp for mentally challenged and neurologically impaired children, has shown me what true goodness really is. Pure souls do exist, and Patrick is one of them. Patrick did not see the differences of skin color among his camp friends or notice that Jimmy came to camp every day wearing the same unwashed clothes. He kissed and hugged everyone just the same and flirtatiously called everyone "boo-tiful." Patrick had the talent of savoring the flavor of each and every moment. No time was wasted with the words "I can't," but rather "We're done already?" He didn't simply come to camp. He *lived* camp. I marveled at his unending energy and his zest for fun.

The "Incredible Hulk" (as he liked to call himself) and I shared a special friendship those unforgettable eight weeks. I taught him the "Electric Slide" and he proudly presented me with hand-picked dandelions each morning. He treasured the shiny star stickers I gave him for being a super dancer. We shared potato chips under the trees at lunch time. Through the sweaty days and the not-so-fun rainy days, we learned from each other. I gave Patrick the feeling that he was wonderful and loved, while he taught me to laugh at the happy and colorful moments that usually flash by without a thought—a kickball game with good friends, the tickle of a horse's whiskers on your cheek, or a piggyback ride in the pool. Patrick had a jack-o-lantern smile for every occasion.

Contrary to the world's standards, I say that Patrick's words really are eloquent. After all, who else could respond to my statement, "I love you very much" with "How many 'verys'?" Every female at camp can surely attest to his unmatched style and charm. His works—the home run in softball, the pencil can in arts and crafts, the "Chicken Dance" lead in our dance finale—were wondrous too, because they were challenges that Patrick met with just a little extra effort. Just a little extra effort, that's all. Way to go, Patrick.

I won't see Patrick until Open House during next year's camp season. We are separated by many miles and find ourselves in two different worlds during the school year. Yet Patrick is with me, inside my head and heart. Sensitive and able to see the decency in everyone, he has touched me and changed me. If the lesson of life is happiness, then I surely have met the most inspiring of teachers. Patrick has taught me to erase the preceding "if."

Essay No. 21

I felt like a cadet at West Point that first week of fifth grade. Mrs. Stith was our sergeant, commanding us to "stand at attention," "walk single file," "keep heads up" and "speak only when spoken to." We had only two rules to obey in her classroom: never talk while Mrs. Stith is talking, and do your homework! We did not dare break these rules, fearing an arduous obstacle course to climb as our consequence or a firing squad awaiting Mrs. Stith's command to release an arsenal of bullets into our bodies.

My fifth-grade mind was not accustomed to such a demanding teacher. Coloring outside the lines, reading *The Great Adventures of Encyclopedia Brown* and building mobiles with construction paper had been the norm. My mouth gaped at the sight of endless reading packets and workbook pages. I was in boot camp now and Mrs. Stith was going to toughen up the troops. Mrs. Stith could see our agony, our pleading eyes hoping she would blow her whistle and let us take a break from the work. But she yelled at the class at any sign of softness. Twenty pages of reading every night kept our stamina up. I cried at the thought of learning how to spell "dictionary," "miserable" and "criminal." I sweated over decimals. How could I learn all this and still have time to watch *Cosby*? This wasn't a youngster's usual anxiety. I honestly thought I hated Mrs. Stith, or "Mrs. Stiff," as we called her, snickering as we pictured our gray-haired tyrant being lowered into a tomb. Who did this old woman think she was anyway, always barking at the class? I had always been the teacher's pet. "Is my work not good enough?" I wondered. How could she destroy my confidence so easily?

"Carrie, how could you get this question wrong?"

"I . . . I . . . don't know," I managed, lowering my head in shame, unable to look at Mrs. Stith's disappointed face.

"Don't you know what a preposition is?"

"Yes, Mrs. Stith," I replied, knowing that this blunder meant K.P. duty. I would have to study my composition book a little extra tonight.

I can't pinpoint exactly why, but sometime during those first few weeks I decided to study hard and make Mrs. Stith proud of me. Maybe I dreamed of following in my older brother's prominent footsteps (some thought they were left by Bigfoot). I wanted to be as studious and intelligent as Christopher. I couldn't destroy the name that my brother and I had established. Mediocrity wasn't part of my vocabulary. I had always been the best in class, favored by my teachers and often chosen to read aloud or go to the chalkboard to do multiplication tables. The difference was that now it didn't come so easily. I would have to work.

Two-page reports turned into detailed posters explaining the formation of igneous, metamorphic, and sedimentary rocks. Mrs. Stith noticed her students' best efforts and rewarded us for hard work with smelly stickers. We loved those stickers and hung them on the wall. One could easily discern my long trail of grapes, strawberries and apples. Reading packets became enjoyable. I left the world of Ramona Quimby and discovered Miss Havisham's mansion, the plummeting guillotine and Jacob Marley's rattling chains. That year marked the beginning of my battle with the nerd syndrome.

Fifth grade helped establish my reputation as a brain. I would skip recess and stay after school just to talk with Mrs. Stith. I would spend hours every night studying beyond the assigned homework. I didn't mind if other kids laughed at me for being studious; they just hadn't met the *real* Mrs. Stith. I no longer saw her as a rigid drill sergeant but rather, a helpful platoon leader. For my part, I was no longer a raw recruit but well on my way to becoming a skilled soldier.

What, in the beginning, were tears of fright and frustration turned to tears of sorrow when I graduated from fifth grade. For graduation Mrs. Stith gave me a special gift—a copy of *A Day No Pigs Would Die*. She wrote on the back cover: "I loved this book. I hope you will too. You are an outstanding girl. Best of luck always. Love, Mrs. Stith." Mrs. Stith retired that year and I never saw my friend again.

Essay No. 22

"Suppose for a moment that I am out walking my beagle and she jumps into the Farmington River down near the bridge and begins to swim across it." Pausing for a moment to allow the class to picture his feeble, obedient beagle escaping from him, Mr. Joffray, affectionately known as "Joff," begins Calculus class. "Now my beagle, being roughly the same age as I, cannot swim very quickly. In fact, she can only swim as fast as the Farmington River's current—about one meter per second. She wants to swim across the Farmington River and end up directly opposite her starting point."

"But Joff, that's impossible," protests Dave, "because to move across she would have to move downstream as well."

After forty-two years at our school, it would be tempting to dismiss Joff's story as ramblings brought on by senility. But such a dismissal would be misleading; Joff was not being senile, he was leading into a class that introduced me to Vectors and Parametric Differentiation. For the last three years, Mr. Joffray has brought math alive for me. Whether figuring out the rate of change of the length of my shadow when walking away from the lamppost outside the library, or imagining Joff's beagle being swept into the torrents of a flooded Connecticut River, Joff never fails to animate advanced calculus.

Inspired by Joff's creative teaching, I hounded the director of student tutoring about becoming a math tutor. After several weeks of awaiting a decision, my hopes of becoming a student tutor had waned. One day, seeing only a single, small sheet of paper about the size of a photo in my mailbox, I thought fleetingly of the worst messages inter-school mail could bring, but I hadn't cut any classes, wasn't having academic problems, and didn't think I had cut too many breakfasts. Student tutoring never crossed my mind. Intrigued, for the note's size ruled out another useless memo about snow days or the new computer network, I twirled in the combination to my mailbox and pulled out the sheet.

"Student Tutoring: Tom Tsing, Algebra II Advanced, Nee Room. Sunday, 4:00." Immediately, I felt a sense of kinship with Tommy. During Freshman year, I too had struggled through Mrs. B's Algebra II Advanced class where her way was *the* way.

Entering the study hall, I knew only the most basic information about Tommy: he was an Asian-born Sophomore who lived in Batch, and this was his first year in the United States. Upon first glance, I saw only the deserted study hall, but in the far corner, hidden almost completely by the odd shadows of the room, a small Asian boy sat stiffly with textbook and notebook aligned neatly in front of him. His textbook seemed to have absorbed his attention; his head was bent over it and even after the door slammed behind me his head never raised. But seeing his expression of bewilderment and his deeply-creased brow, I hurried over to the table.

"Hi. My name is Nat. Are you Tommy?"

He stood quickly, stiffly extended his arm, and haltingly said, "Hello my name is Tommy Tsing. Pleased to meet you," confirming my suspicion that Tommy's problem was twofold: not only did he have trouble with the math, but he also struggled to understand English. That Sunday progressed as every other would: Tommy produced from his neatly-organized binder Mrs. B's immaculate syllabus and I taught the concept-of-the-week. We met again on Tuesday to review homework and on Thursday to prepare for the weekly test.

As the term progressed, much of my enjoyment came because Tommy's face lit up with understanding more frequently, indicating that he was learning. But the learning was not limited to Tommy; I, too, was learning. I learned that what is being taught is not nearly as important as how it is being taught. Unfailingly, whenever I was able to enliven material by making it humorous or by applying it to a real-life situation that could be imagined, Tommy's comprehension skyrocketed. And when Tommy moved from a C at the midterm to a B+ by the end of the trimester, I was proud to have played a part in his success. But perhaps the most gratifying part of tutoring Tommy was that I was able to emphasize presentation again and again, whether tutoring inner-city Hartford elementary students or learning the second half of Calculus BC largely on my own.

"So what's the topic this week?"

"Vectors and Pro . . ." Tommy stammered.

"Here let me see . . . Oh, Vectors and Projectile Motion . . . say, do you know Mr. Joffray, Tommy?"

"No."

"Well, have you ever seen an old guy, who sort of limps a little, walking his really old dog early in the morning?"

"Yes."

"Now imagine if his dog ran away from him one morning . . . and jumped in the Farmington River . . . and started to swim to the other side."

. . . And Tommy smiled imagining this ridiculous spectacle.

WORLD VIEWS AND PERSONAL CONVICTIONS *(8 Essays)*

Essay No. 23

> "I'm sorry," said the tree,
> "but I have no money.
> I have only leaves and apples.
> But take my apples . . ."
> *The Giving Tree*, by Shel Silverstein

December 15th. Ms. Lorri Kellogg, founder of the non-profit adoption agency Universal Aid for Children Inc., attended my high school's Human Rights Conference and addressed the deplorable conditions of infants and teenage orphans in war-torn third-world countries. She began with a video of Romania which showed children eating from garbage cans, infants in worn-out cloth diapers, and teenagers in their last months of pregnancy. The overwhelming horror of the scenes appalled me. While I sat comfortably, surrounded by classmates who live sheltered lives, there in front of me was the sullen face of a 17-year-old who looked as if her only savior were death. It broke my heart to discover that, at the dawn of the 21st century, countless orphans were enduring such deprivation and humiliating misfortune. Then, I realized that pity was useless if not followed by action, and I decided to initiate the first high school Universal Aid for Children Reach Out Organization. Subsequent events significantly shaped the essence of who I am today.

The steps necessary to form the organization were challenging; however, with patience and dedication, I prevailed. Ms. Kellogg suggested that I sponsor the country with the most severe problems, and after extensive research I chose El Salvador. Afterwards, I organized a group of thirty-five motivated students and began fundraising efforts and clothing drives. We then wrote letters to the First Lady of El

Salvador, hoping to convey our enthusiasm for effecting positive change.

The work involved has been demanding; however, the results and commendations received have been remarkable. After dedicating 600 hours to Reach Out, I was invited by Ms. Kellogg to accompany her to El Salvador to meet the First Lady on October 21st. I am thrilled by this prestigious honor and determined to help the government make reforms within the orphan institutions. In preparation, I recently met with Mrs. Mylene Alvergue, vice-consul of El Salvador in Miami, and expressed the following goals: to furnish the institutions with professional and medical provisions and to enhance the areas of hygiene, education, and health care. Ms. Alvergue agreed and suggested that I inform the First Lady of my intentions.

What do I hope to accomplish by a single visit to a third-world country in the midst of economic despair? What can one small group of high-school students do to institute significant reforms in the face of extreme deprivation? In examining these questions, I believe that information is power. After I assess first-hand the children's most dire needs, I am confident that I will be able to improve their lives. Yes, we are a handful of teenagers facing an enormous challenge; but, we can begin a legacy of hope that will evolve into something greater than all of us. As evidenced in *The Giving Tree*, the desire to give of myself is all I have to offer, but I can rest in the satisfaction of knowing that some day soon lives will be touched in a positive way because I chose not to accept reality.

Essay No. 24

I live in a small suburban town, where the atmosphere is slowly being destroyed by the influx of commercial business and development. A great source of anxiety to me is the extent to which this may eradicate the town's heritage and environment . . .

A cool evening breeze wafted over the age-old former municipal court, illuminated by a stately street lamp from the late nineteenth century. Through the rhythmic, dreary swaying of two tall willows, one could perceive the building's simple architecture: four perpendicular walls and a sharply pitched roof. Windows were few and unadorned. The single magnificent feature of the court was a towering steeple, evidence of its early service as a Protestant church. Once, children and their parents gathered there in their best attire for Sunday sermons. Now, the ancient edifice stood silent, a lifeless presence dwarfed by the vastness of the cloudy sky. As the clouds drifted, a glimmer of moonlight fell on the building, lighting the hallway within. The corridor was enveloped in white, from the porcelain tiles to the alabaster walls. Two antique benches, crafted from mahogany, stood at either end of the hall, their splendor obscured by a thick layer of dust.

A few minutes later, the main door creaked open, and the street lamp projected onto the hallway the silhouette of a lone, plain-looking man. He moved confidently through the court-house, since after his duty in the army he had served as magistrate within these walls. Moving toward one of the four inner doors, he thrust it open with flamboyance, admiring his former office with the strength of a thousand memories. Thoughtfully, he continued to his chair and sat down. Taking up the gavel, he smiled; the furnishings in the room had neither been replaced nor refurbished since its construction, and they remained as solid as the day they had been made. Poised upon his former judicial post, he relived his favorite cases. Most were neighborly quarrels or property disputes, and none were as brutal as those he was hearing about these days. Disturbed by these thoughts, the man arose and moved toward the door once more, and after swiftly passing through the corridor, he left the building. As he exited, he felt something bound over his foot. Since winter was approaching, he believed it was probably a squirrel hoarding food; reaching into his coat pocket, he produced a half-eaten sandwich, bent down, and placed it on the clayish ground for the animal, should it return.

An hour later, a black, polished oxford crushed that sandwich, and the brilliant glow of a lantern flooded the small courthouse. The man who loomed in the doorway was nattily dressed: the suit he sported was expertly tailored, his overcoat was of the finest wool, and his elegant hat was tilted back at a dashing angle. He was young, no more than thirty years of age, and he walked quickly through the hall, glancing around furtively and taking deep breaths from a smoldering menthol. Lackadaisically sliding into a bench, he stirred up the age-old dust, which rose quickly around him. Irritated, he continued to move about, scrutinizing the rooms. The furnishings, he thought, would bring quite a sum through auction, as would the oil paintings on the walls—portraits of men who had contributed to the community. Then he could bring in a blasting crew to level the building. He found the court's history to be of passing interest but was deeply attracted to the profitability of building a shopping center on the land.

Content with his plans, he pictured himself a dozen times richer and smiled approvingly to himself. As he turned to depart, he noticed a half-destroyed window and decided to end its misery. With a swift and brutal kick, he shattered the remaining glass, rending a spider's web in the process. Approaching the door, he turned off the switch that gave power to the street lamp; no sense in wasting electricity and, therefore, money. He casually dropped his cigarette on the tiled floor and stamped it out with his heel. Heading for his car, he murmured to himself that the trees would have to be cut down to extend the parking lot. That would cost a fair amount, but he hoped that selling the lumber would pay for most of it. Getting into his sedan, he looked around and wondered why people had lobbied against his venture; after all, it could only bring the town revenue. Then there was the roar of a Buick six-cylinder, and as its drone dissipated into nothingness, silence descended upon the courthouse once again, to remain until the demolition crew arrived the following morning.

Essay No. 25

[This essay was accompanied by a photograph of a saddle shoe taken by the applicant during a trip to Poland.]

I wore saddle shoes five days a week for nine years of my life. I started Kindergarten with the clunky leather ones that were most common and did not think much about them. In the third grade I had grown to hate my uniform and, like all my friends, tried to find the lightest, most un-saddle-shoe-like saddle shoe. I wore what I could find, plastic blue and white imitations, until the sixth grade. Then it became popular to wear the old style, clunky, black heavy, hard leather again. In the eighth grade my classmates and I signed our good-byes on our shoes, and I wore my saddle shoes home from the last day of grammar school with a heavy heart. Now I wear those saddle shoes as a fashion statement, but they serve more as a gentle reminder of old school friends the years have left behind.

The shoe in this picture is not mine. When I took this shot, however, it certainly felt like it belonged to me. During the spring of my sophomore year, I spent a week in Poland visiting concentration camps followed by a week of sight-seeing in Israel. I was accompanied by seven-thousand Jewish students, Rabbis, teachers, and Holocaust survivors from all over the world. Together we made up "The March of the Living," an annual program run by the Bureau of Jewish Education in which students from around the world meet in Poland and Israel to witness Holocaust Remembrance Day and Israeli Independence Day.

On my final day in Poland I entered the gates of Majdonek concentration camp, only a few hours away from the village where my grandparents had lived. I took this picture there, at the back of an old barrack that has been converted into a museum. I thought of my family then; my heritage and beliefs. I realized that for nine years a shoe had identified who I was, and now I was barefoot. I was only what my past had made me, and over fifty years ago another girl had a similar definition. This tie came not just because of our shoes, but because of our religion and our love for it.

Years ago a girl wore that saddle shoe to school. She marveled at its heavy weight and saw her friends walking in matching pairs. Unfortunately, looking at the bright white leather amid the faded brown of loafers, heels, and lace-ups, I knew that girl's fate all too well. They had taken those shoes from her. They had taken her. And I was thankful to have my own pair waiting in my closet across the world; thankful for my family, their love, and our tradition.

Essay No. 26

In the Spring of my freshman year I was invited to travel to Albany, New York, to lobby for increased school aid for the New York state budget. While this was a memorable experience, it was what happened on the bus ride home that affected the rest of my high-school years.

The bus was filled with about thirty passengers. A diverse mixture of students, teachers, parents, and administrators. Somehow the conversation turned to the lack of AIDS education in the health curriculum. The talk led to the formation of a committee. The South Huntington School District AIDS Committee was born with twelve members. Of the four student members I was the only freshman.

The Committee visited schools, heard speakers, and discussed frightening statistics about the deadly disease of AIDS. The universal reaction was: "How could this disease affect a small suburban community like ours?" We came to the realization that AIDS could affect anyone, anywhere, anytime. Should we write to the state education department and request a review of the curriculum? Maybe we could just have a lecturer come to the school. After much deliberation we decided to implement an AIDS Peer Education Program. Our goal: for our high-school students to "teach" our junior-high students. That summer we gathered forty sophomores, juniors, and seniors to "train." For five days we went through rigorous training. We learned all about AIDS, teen pregnancy, STD's, and condom use. We also learned how to present the material in an orderly manner.

School began and we continued our training during weekly evening meetings. It was in February that the true test began. Each pair of "peer educators" was assigned to a seventh-grade health class. At first it was difficult. Each time my partner or I said "vaginal secretion" the class would break into laughter. [We broke into laughter too the first three or four times . . . okay, maybe eight or nine times.] Toward the last two lessons it seemed like some of what we were saying was actually sinking in. I was having a great time while teaching these kids. In one role-playing exercise I played a guy who was trying to get his girlfriend to have sex with him. My partner played the girlfriend. Every pair of eyes was glued to our acting, not because it was Oscar caliber, but because the kids associated with the situation.

The program was a great success that year and an even greater success the next year when the district granted permission to extend the program to include ninth-grade science classes. By this time, I was the only student left on the AIDS Committee. All the other students had graduated, and I took on an even greater role in the program. When we visited PTA meetings and Board of Education meetings, I spoke for the group. I represented our AIDS group as a member of the 1995 Teen Health Conference Planning Board. When we won an award for having one of the best AIDS programs in our county, I accepted it on behalf of our school.

The AIDS program took on a special meaning to me. As we enter the third year of the program, I'm the only student who has been there from the start. Throughout my four years of high school, I have devoted many hours to the success of our program. I am proud of my work, and I am even prouder of the fact that our program is saving lives.

Essay No. 27

I have often wondered whether the United States has an obligation to get involved in the internal conflicts of other countries. When does the power to intervene become an obligation to act? I gained some insight into this dilemma when a small part of the Bosnian war spilled into my home last year.

During the height of the Bosnian conflict, my family was informed that twenty Bosnian students were airlifted out of the mountains surrounding Sarajevo. A relief organization called "Bridge for Humanity" sought families in the United States that would take in these Muslim teenagers for the school year. The need was urgent because the U.S. government would not let them board planes until homes had been found.

My parents and I spent at least a week contemplating whether we should offer. At first I resisted, fearing the obligations that I would be forced to undertake. I knew it would be my job to help this visitor integrate with the students at our school and to look out for him in social situations. Eventually, my parents agreed, but they left the final decision to me. The deciding factor was my parents' reminder of the six-million people who were killed in World War II. Many of these Jews, gypsies, and other "undesirables" had tried to flee Germany and Eastern Europe, but found no country that would accept them. Being Jewish, I found it easy to imagine how desperate I would have been in the same situation, needing someone to rescue me. The choice was made.

Emir arrived last October with one small bag. He told us that he had crawled out of Sarajevo through a narrow tunnel leading to the mountains beyond the city. He crawled for many hours in this hot confined space, terrified of being caught and shot by the Serbs. I doubt that Emir looked back during this journey. The building where he had once lived had been blown up months before. He survived in cellars, with little food, and electricity for only five hours each week. Behind Emir, the bombs fell on his city every day.

When Emir arrived at my house, for the first day he could not stop smiling. He appeared jovial and appreciative of the United States and of my family. Soon, however, it became clear that Emir had not escaped Bosnia completely. His inner rage began to emerge. His hatred of the Serbs permeated his thoughts and judgments. Eventually, he began to hate the United States too. To Emir, America's failure to prevent Serbian atrocities made it evil. He found it reprehensible that some Americans opposed sending troops to defend the Bosnian minorities. He hated Americans that would not risk their lives to save his people.

The six months that Emir lived in my home are the most difficult that I can remember. Many nights I would stay up very late talking to him about his negative attitude toward the United States. As he attacked our society, I found myself becoming defensive, then angry. When my mother found butcher knives hidden in his drawers, anger turned to fear. I began to understand the depth of the trauma Emir had experienced in Bosnia, even as I pulled away from him. I discovered some limits to what I could give.

It is now six months later. I have learned that the casualties of war cannot be measured merely by life and death. Those who survive may live with pain, and those who try to help may feel its repercussions. This experience brought a new dimension to my life, as well as a new appreciation of my advantages in the United States. As we are a privileged nation, I feel we have an obligation to aid both oppressed and impoverished countries. There are risks, there are rewards, and there are degrees of failure. Sometimes those we help may hate us for being less than they imagined. But because we did not look away when we were needed and had something to give, we have lived up to our moral obligation.

Essay No. 28

I close my eyes and can still hear her—the little girl with a voice so strong and powerful we could hear her halfway down the block. She was a Russian peasant who asked for money and in return gave the only thing she had—her voice. I paused outside a small shop and listened. She brought to my mind the image of Little Orphan Annie. I could not understand the words she sang, but her voice begged for attention. It stood out from the noises of Arbat Street, pure and impressive, like the chime of a bell. She sang from underneath an old-style lamp post in the shadow of a building, her arms extended and head thrown back. She was small and of unremarkable looks. Her brown hair escaped the bun it had been pulled into, and she occasionally reached up to remove a stray piece from her face. Her clothing I can't recall. Her voice, on the other hand, is permanently imprinted on my mind.

I asked one of the translators about the girl. Elaina told me that she and hundreds of others like her throughout the former Soviet Union add to their families' income by working on the streets. The children are unable to attend school, and their parents work full-time. These children know that the consequence of an unsuccessful day is no food for the table. Similar situations occurred during the Depression in the United

States, but those American children were faceless shoeshine boys of the twenties. This girl was real to me.

When we walked past her I gave her money. It was not out of pity but rather admiration. Her smile of thanks did not interrupt her singing. The girl watched us as we walked down the street. I know this because when I looked back she smiled again. We shared that smile, and I knew I would never forget her courage and inner strength. She was only a child, yet was able to pull her own weight during these uncertain times. On the streets of Moscow, she used her voice to help her family survive. For this "Annie," there is no Daddy Warbucks to come to the rescue. Her salvation will only come when Russia and its people find prosperity.

Essay No. 29

On April 15, 1947, a man strode out to first base at Ebbets Field in Brooklyn, a black man wearing Dodger blue. This was Jackie Robinson, a significant figure for a number of reasons, but the one that made him so special was his absolute inequality. The inequity of his position in the arena of race set him apart, and his superior abilities as a ball player placed him a rung above his contemporaries. That is the essence of rewarding performance—to raise one person above the pack, to place him in a more esteemed position so that we can all learn from him, learn to emulate him, and learn to pull ourselves out of the quagmire of mediocrity and reach his height.

Growth and evolution proceed in a stepwise fashion, and while equality is obviously the loftiest goal toward which we can strive, transforming individuals into role models is how we better ourselves. Otherwise, we muddle along in our brief existence, not having exacted any change, not having accomplished anything.

Not everyone can be singled out, however, for if we all have our own particular agendas without any form of unity, then our society cannot progress together. What we must do, then, is to balance individual achievement with the needs of the group and identify barriers that separate us as a people so that we can break them down. We can be equal and excellent at the same time, insofar as we are equal in our goal to emulate the accomplishments of an individual role model. In Jackie Robinson's time, America was practically united in its aversion to integration. He became an icon, and this country took a hard look at itself. Sometimes a little inequality helps.

Essay No. 30

I had a mental image of them standing there, wearing ragged clothes, hot and depressed, looking upon us as intruders in their world. They would sneer at our audacity. We would invade their territory only to take pictures and observe them like tourists.

We climbed out of the van and faced eleven men assembled in the shade. My mental image was confirmed. My class, consisting of twelve primarily white, middle-class students, felt out of place. Our Politics of Food curriculum at Governor's School, a summer environmental program, included an interview with migrant workers. We were at a farm worker labor camp in southern New Jersey, but judging from the rural landscape, it may as well have been Iowa. I felt like a trespasser.

So we were surprised when one man—the oldest of the group—approached and offered each of us a piece of candy. The man appeared remarkably coarse; his beige skin was leathery like a crocodile's, and yellow teeth jutted from his gum line. His shoddy turquoise tee-shirt and blue jeans conveyed a sense of basic humanity. His broken English was barely discernible. Fortunately, a man wearing a nearly clean denim shirt and jeans stepped forward to interpret.

Contrary to my preconceptions, the men seemed glad to see us. They bantered and joked like office staff on a coffee break. They told of their isolation and the rarity of meeting other people, let alone students. They seemed genuinely interested in helping our study. Just as we asked about their backgrounds, they questioned us about ours. "Do any of you have jobs?" asked one worker.

The old man told us his story as we all walked around the fields. He was sixty-eight, had immigrated from Colombia at a young age, and had been working at this labor camp for almost twenty years. Long since divorced, he had been performing unskilled labor all his life. The younger workers conveyed similar stories. They generally had a high-school education and moved to the United States for financial reasons. I was surprised that one man in his twenties had a girlfriend in New York, drove a taxi half the year, and hoped to attend college soon. Their lives put our teen anxiety in perspective. Sure, we may become upset when the car is taken away for the weekend. We may be preoccupied with wearing the right clothes. Yet these men had nowhere to go on Saturday nights. They wore dirty, shabby attire. And it did not matter.

Before we left, the old man picked twelve small cucumbers and proudly gave them to the class. I had never enjoyed eating cucumbers before. But since then I have become quite fond of them.

LESSONS LEARNED, SETBACKS, AND SUCCESSES *(6 Essays)*

Essay No. 31

I walked into the first class that I have ever taught and confronted utter chaos. The four students in my Latin class were engaged in a heated spitball battle. They were all following the lead of Andrew, a tall eleven-year-old African-American boy.

Andrew turned to me and said, "Why are we learning Latin if no one speaks it? This a waste of time."

I broke out in a cold sweat. I thought, "How on Earth am I going to teach this kid?"

It was my first day of Summerbridge, a nationwide collaborative of thirty-six public and private high schools. Its goal is to foster a desire to learn in young, underprivileged students, while also exposing college and high-school students to teaching. Since I enjoy tutoring, I decided to apply to the program. I thought to myself, "Teaching can't be that difficult. I can handle it." I have never been more wrong in my life.

After what seemed like an eternity, I ended that first class feeling as though I had accomplished nothing. Somehow I needed to catch Andrew's attention. For the next two weeks, I tried everything from indoor chariot races to a Roman toga party, but nothing seemed to work.

During the third week, after I had exhausted all of my ideas, I resorted to a game that my Latin teacher had used. A leader yells out commands in Latin and the students act out the commands. When I asked Andrew to be the leader, I found the miracle that I had been seeking. He thought it was great that he could order the teacher around with commands such as "jump in place" and "touch the window." I told him that if he asked me in Latin to do something, I would do it as long as he would do the same. With this agreement, I could teach him new words outside the classroom, and he could make his teacher hop on one foot in front of his friends. Andrew eventually gained a firm grasp of Latin.

Family night occurred during the last week of Summerbridge. We explained to the parents what we had accomplished. At the conclusion, Andrew's mom thanked me for teaching him Latin. She said, "Andrew wanted to speak Latin with someone, so he taught his younger brother."

My mouth fell open. I tempered my immediate desire to utter, "Andrew did what?" I was silent for a few seconds as I tried to regain my composure, but when I responded, I was unable to hide my surprise.

That night I remembered a comment an English teacher had made to me. I had asked her, "Why did you become a teacher?"

She responded with a statement that perplexed me at the time. She said, "There is nothing greater than empowering someone with the love of knowledge." Now, I finally understood what she meant.

When I returned to Summerbridge for my second summer, the first words out of Andrew's mouth were, "Is there going to be a Latin class this year?"

Essay No. 32

This much I remember: my mother walking into my room and saying the six words which changed my views of people and my own actions forever—"You made him cry, you know." Brief moments of that day rise and fall in my memory, with certain portions crystal clear and other parts shrouded in mystery. Yet no matter how much of the story I can accurately recall, I will never forget this one phrase. But to avoid getting ahead of myself, I should start at the beginning.

I was rocking back and forth on the swingset behind my house next to Mark Kramer. Mark had always been bigger than I. He had also, for as long as I could remember, been my friend. From those earliest pre-school days at The Training Depot, we were inseparable. I don't recall how or why we became fast friends, but I do know that some of my earliest and fondest memories come from the days I spent with him.

It was not for Mark's size that I respected him most, but more for all of the qualities that he possessed which I lacked. He was braver than I ever thought I could be and more comfortable talking to people, especially girls. His sense of humor never failed him, and he always managed to make everyone laugh. Yet, although he made many friends over the years I knew him, he never deserted me. This is why it hurt me so much the day my mom told me the outcome of my actions.

We were well into one of our insult wars which we waged whenever our parents were out of the room. We never took it seriously, at least not until that day. We were both very quick thinkers, and to us the "war" had been simply a warped means of recreation. But on this day, Mark dug out the heavy artillery—an insult book. As a result, I was forced beyond the old standbys into more original forms of cut-downs. No "your mother" cracks would hold up against him today. No, I was in for a fight, and shortly after we began, I realized I was losing. I admit that I began to panic, and I was reaching for something, anything, which would act as a final, crushing blow. In a daze, I blurted out, "Oh yeah?! Well you stutter!"

I did not think much about the comment at the time. For one thing, it made me the clear victor. That one phrase shut him up for good. Sure it was mean, attacking him in the one weak spot which we both knew he had but never spoke of. We were playing around, or so I thought. Mark soon left to go home, uneventfully, and in defeat. I did not think that I would ever hear of it again and had put it completely out of mind until my mother came into my room later that night to tell me what I had done.

Five words . . . and realization. Suddenly, a shocking image appeared in my mind. I envisioned this boy, my first true friend and the first person outside of my family that I respected, hunched over and weeping. This brief moment, which I had brushed off as nothing, affected Mark profoundly, and I had not even realized it. I claimed to be Mark's friend, but I had been blind to the pain which he experienced as a result of his minor speech impediment. To me, the comment had been a joke, but to him it had been an insult harsher than any other. And it had cut this brave, imposing boy more than I could have imagined.

Of course I apologized immediately and I told him that I had not known what the impact of my actions would be. And, as is often the case with childhood friendships, all was soon forgiven. However, at least as far as I was concerned, all was not forgotten. Although Mark eventually stopped stuttering and later moved to Cleveland, I have often replayed that moment in my mind. For me, it serves as a reminder of the terrible power that I can have over another person's feelings and of the need for analyzing my words before I speak.

But finally, and most importantly, this moment showed me what it was to needlessly hurt another human being. I realized that as easy as it is to make someone feel awful, it is just as easy to make him or her feel terrific. Since that time, I have made an effort to spare people from experiencing pointless pain from my words and actions. Mark Kramer probably does not remember the day I made him cry. But I have never been able to forget it: the flippant attitude I had when I told him of his flaw, the shock I felt when I learned of the result, and the decision I made to see that it would never happen again.

Essay No. 33

Ten years from now Tim Dickson won't even remember my name. The unknowing recipient of my undying love for two years, Tim had been everything a girl could ever ask for:

smart, handsome, witty, athletic, with a voice that could make angels weep. Everyone knew his name. To a shy little country mouse, nearly invisible in our student body, he was the epitome of manliness. I sat in my corner of room C-119 and gazed adoringly at his profile as he amazed the class of Modern World History with his dashing style. Carefully planning the routes to my classes to coincide with his, I was his silent shadow.

After fourteen months, contrary to my hopes, Tim still was not aware of my existence. Determined to bring myself to his attention, I staged my entrance to his heart with all the flair I could muster. I would breach his defenses at the next history oral presentation in the guise of the dashing Cardinal Richelieu.

It was now or never! Striding into the classroom, my head raised, eyes flashing, I stood proudly, the colors of my eighteenth-century costume catching the light and giving me courage. My opening line shook with tight emotion. "Gentlemen, I am disgusted!" My voice alternately lashed out in rage and purred in soft persuasion. I gloried in my elocution. Each word was power. My voice rose to a brilliant conclusion, and I stood with my arms outstretched and my head bowed in submission.

Dead silence.

My left knee trembled uncontrollably. Why did no one speak? My hands began to shake so I pulled them behind me—like one condemned. My eyes gauged the distance to the door.

Then someone began to clap. More joined in. Tim looked into my eyes—and smiled. He smiled!

Joy, oh joy. My soul overflowed with rapture. I had done it! He noticed me! All the shame, all the worry, and all the castagation melted away in that moment. I knew how to make him love me. I simply had to speak better, sing better, act better, and write better than anyone else.

Determined, I joined competitions, played in concerts, and wrote essays that were read in class. When Tim transferred to the A.P. class, so did I. I threw myself into class discussions, attempting to dazzle him with my intelligence and intrepidity. Making friends with his friends, I dogged his steps.

The next summer Tim moved away. I never heard from him again. But the transformation in me had taken place. Now I was involved for the simple pleasure of being involved. Challenging people surrounded me. Biff taught me to love. Dave taught me to laugh. Ramez taught me to break my limits. Alit gave me confidence. Whenever I was in danger of reverting to a wallflower, one of my new friends would drag me into another club or activity.

In every foray into the threatening world of "school activities," I still feel an overpowering impulse to run. But although my feelings haven't changed, my actions have. My stomach still tightens when I enter a room of unfamiliar faces, but I walk in. I still want to run from risk and recrimination, but I keep my feet firmly planted.

Tim Dickson was the single best thing that ever happened to me, all because he didn't know me from Adam.

Essay No. 34

I want to learn to take risks. I want to change my attitude about taking chances. Assessing my academic and extracurricular achievements, I am proud of my accomplishments. I see myself as an open-minded, goal-oriented person who achieves and succeeds through hard work and determination. How much of that success is a result of staying on comfortable ground?

I began wondering about the range of my abilities when I attended Northwestern University's Theater Arts Program last summer. The theme of the institute, announced by the director, was: "Dare to fail gloriously." This idea encouraged participants to take bold risks on the stage. Over time I applied this philosophy to my acting and my life. I began the Northwestern program as a quasi-accomplished actress with a hunger to absorb all I could about acting. I emerged not only a well-rounded thespian, but also a more secure person with a new outlook. I knew that there was something about my life that I wanted to change and could change. Now, as I approach college, I am committed to continuing successes and occasional glorious failures.

The first day at Northwestern I was asked to choose among three subjects in technical theater, ranking them in order of preference. Set Design was my first choice, followed by Costumes, and finally Stage Lighting. Much to my dismay, I was assigned to the lighting crew. Though disappointed, I tried to stay open-minded. I knew nothing about lighting, but followed the slogan which kept repeating in my head: "Dare to fail. . . ."

By the third lighting session, I had discovered a new passion: I was eager to learn everything I could about lights. Having always been a performer who enjoyed the limelight, I had never realized the skill required to create it properly. In my free time I climbed the catwalks, memorized cues, circuited lamps, or changed gels. My competence was recognized when I was selected head light board operator for the final production of the summer.

If the choice to study lighting had not been made for me, I would have missed an enriching opportunity. The experience taught me to take more risks, rather than to follow the most certain path to success. The exposure made me realize how limited my perspective had been in approaching new situations. The choice that was made for me, undesirable as it seemed at the outset, taught me to embrace new experiences and ideas.

I believe that "the past is prologue." In college I will take more risks, convinced that the potential rewards outweigh my fear of failure. I have stopped trying to select a major, and am committed to studying in many academic disciplines before deciding on a field of concentration.

Accepting the possibility of failure is a new concept for me. While I have had recognition for academics, performing arts, community service, and athletic achievements, perhaps I have missed some enriching experiences because my certainty of success was doubtful. I will not avoid such opportunities in the future since I am changing my philosophy of life: I am learning to take risks.

Essay No. 35

For many years, I have had difficulty concentrating on my schoolwork. Although my parents provided me with a private-school education and with tutors, I still didn't achieve the grades that I desired even though I was highly motivated. Therefore, I welcomed my parents' invitation to visit a doctor who could evaluate me to see if there was a physical basis for my difficulties. When I was finally diagnosed with Attention Deficit Disorder (ADD), I had mixed emotions. At first, I was relieved that the condition had been identified and that I could obtain treatment and learn to overcome this handicap. However, I was not pleased to have a condition that interfered with my learning. The challenge of learning to live with and conquer ADD provides me with daily insights into myself.

Before I realized there was a possibility that I had a learning disability, I was very insecure about my intelligence level. I couldn't grasp concepts that were taught in class, so I often gave up and allowed myself to daydream. I would study for tests and take notes, yet when I got my scores back, they weren't what I expected. I felt incapable of ever doing well, no matter how hard I tried. I came to the conclusion that this problem was not my fault, and I didn't know how to deal with it.

When the doctor told me I had ADD and he could prescribe medications to help, I was upset. Whenever I had heard of others who had ADD, I had always regarded them negatively. I had the impression that they were people who were never going to amount to anything because they were limited in ability. Even though my doctor informed me that this wasn't true, I still felt embarrassed. I planned not to tell anyone, not even my sisters. Furthermore, I was worried that I might have to be on medication for the rest of my life.

After a series of discussions with my parents and my doctor, I had the choice of using the medicine Ritalin or dealing with problem on my own. My doctor explained that the medicine was not a crutch, but an aid. It wasn't going to make me smarter or force me to concentrate involuntarily; I still had to make a conscious effort to focus on my work. Since I had been dealing with my unknown problem by myself, I decided to try the Ritalin. The only people who knew were my parents and my tutor, and I planned to keep it that way.

It has been six months since I was diagnosed with ADD, and my views have changed drastically. My theory that everyone with ADD is ignorant has been proven wrong. My doctor informed me that more people than I thought had ADD, and some are even adults with prestigious jobs. He also said that I should never be insecure about my intelligence. It was as if I had been doing my work with one hand tied behind my back; now with a little aid, my hands were untied! Most important, I am improving in my schoolwork and maintaining a better relationship with my friends.

Once I realized that dealing with my learning problem was helping my life, I no longer had a problem. I understand that I shouldn't be ashamed of something that can't be helped. I have enough self-confidence to know that it is all right to be different. Indeed, I have learned an important lesson about self-perception: It's not what we think of ourselves; rather, it's what we *make* of ourselves that matters.

Essay No. 36

"They look alike, they walk alike, at times they even talk alike." That's the theme from the old *Patty Duke Show* and was, I thought, the theme for the people of Lafayette, California. I moved from Oakland to Lafayette when I was in the seventh grade, and I found that I was doing more than moving over the hill. I was moving from a city brimming with diversity to a place where everyone seemed ominously similar. At age twelve I was facing the challenge of how and whether to fit in.

Every day was a struggle for me. Being new at a school was trying enough, but attempting to be an individual at a new school was virtually inconceivable. I tried to be bizarre to gain attention and win friends, but I ended up the subject of everyone's extended index finger and of countless whispers and laughs. A few people sympathized with me and did their best to help me. To them I was and still am grateful. Others, however, did their best to ridicule me. These people had a lasting effect on my life that, eventually, would aid me.

In high school I discovered an important outlet that would reshape my attitude and my mind—drama. I enrolled in Drama 1 the first year I was eligible to do so, and I became president of the Drama Club. I somehow got the lead in the school play, Thornton Wilder's *Our Town*. I also appeared in a small theater company's production of *Guys and Dolls*. Performing brought me great pleasure and enhanced my growing confidence. The next year I landed the lead in the school play again and participated in two plays at a community theater. I entered the improvisation competition at the college and won, shocking myself. I had gained an identity. I was an actor.

When I step on stage, the first minute is agony. My throat is dry. My breathing is unsteady and sweat drips down my back. I am terrified. I love it. To me, it doesn't matter if a play is great. Just the thrill of getting up on stage as another person is incredible. When I perform in front of a crowd, I want to make the audience care. I want to exhaust them with my passion so that they leave discussing the play. I want to help the players on stage with me to be better actors. I want to be an actor whose characters seem so real that they cause discomfort or insight, joy or sadness.

I found myself using life experience as a major contributor to my drama. The people I hated for their teasing at intermediate school became very valuable. When I need to dislike someone or something in a role, I bring all those people to mind. When I need to feel grateful to someone, I think of the choice few who wanted to help me. Emotions are easy to evoke with the proper stimuli.

Although the move to the land of clones at age twelve seemed like a personal hell at first, perhaps it was for the best. If I had not been surrounded by what I perceived as anonymity, I might not have found out who I really was. Now I have the opportunity to become anyone. Acting has given me a chance to become whomever I please. What more could I want? Mom, Dad, the move seemed like a questionable idea, but thank you for forcing it upon me. It turned out to be the opportunity of my lifetime.

PREOCCUPATIONS AND PASSIONS
(7 Essays)

Essay No. 37

I am an addict. I tell people I could stop anytime, but deep inside, I know I am lying. I need to listen to music, to write music, to play music every day. I can't go a whole day without, at the very least, humming or whistling the tunes that crowd my head. I sing myself hoarse each morning in the shower, and playing the trumpet leaves a red mouthpiece-shaped badge of courage on my lips all day. I suspect that if someone were to look at my blood under a microscope, they would see, between the platelets and t-cells, little black musical notes coursing through my body.

On many occasions I've woken my family (and perhaps the neighborhood) composing on the piano early in the morning. Other times, my mother will admonish, "It's too late to play the trumpet." But I can't understand why people wouldn't want to hear music any time of the day. Keeping the music bottled up is more than I can bear. "I never worry about you sneaking up on me," my friend once admitted to me. "I've never seen you walking without humming or whistling to yourself."

For me, playing the trumpet is the opiate of music in its purest form. I love to play in all types of ensembles. I'm not just addicted to one kind of music; I couldn't imagine limiting myself like that. Choosing just one kind of music would be worse than choosing one food to eat for the rest of my life. Playing orchestral music, for example, I become a sharp-shooter. Waiting, I hide behind rows of string players, ready to jump out with a staccato attack that pierces the hearts of the audience. Playing in an orchestra, I can be Atlas, holding the other musicians above my head, or Icarus, flying through a solo in a desperate attempt to reach the heavens.

Completely different, small jazz ensembles are like a conversation with your closest friends. "So," someone asks, "what do you think about. . . ." We mull it over together, and then each has a say. I build on what the piano proclaimed, or disagree with the saxophone. Playing jazz like this makes me giddy; jazz musicians know that music isn't little dots on a piece of paper, but a feeling that makes you want to stomp your feet, shout for joy, or grab a partner and swing. Taking a solo, I extend my wings, a baby bird jumping out of my nest for the first time. Flapping madly, I hope that by some act of seeming magic my music will fly on its own.

Not only am I an addict, I am also a pusher. The schools in the neighboring community are unable to afford musical instruction, so each week several other high school musicians and I teach music at an elementary school on the east side of town. I work with all of the trumpets for an hour before we join the other instruments to play as a band. Having tutored since freshman year, I've seen my students gradually improve. Four years ago, few of them could read music.

This year, one of my best students won a scholarship to the Stanford Jazz Workshop. Many students from the east side of town never continue on through high school. At our last homecoming game, all of my students came and played with the pep band. One student, who had been struggling in school, confided in me that playing with us had made him excited about attending high school for the first time. That afternoon, I saw a new music addiction forming; it was almost better than being hooked myself.

Essay No. 38

My second home doesn't actually exist, tangibly. It's a hidden corner on the vast electronic world of the information superhighway: America Online's Simulation City.

I've always preferred the world of fantasy to that of reality. It's why I write, and why I act, and why I've been nicknamed "bookworm" more times than I can count. So when I saw the notice last January about a new weekly role-playing game forming on-line, it was only natural for me to check it out. I'd never role-played before, not so much as a round of Dungeons & Dragons, and I was curious. When I "stepped" into the chatroom that first Thursday night ten months ago, I had no idea what to expect. What I found was a community of bright, imaginative people who, like me, never quite fit into the real world.

There's Sandra, a newlywed who keeps us updated on the "joys of matrimony" and the antics of her husband—like the new color he created when he threw all her clothes into the washer at once. We all nearly died of jealously the night she missed the "sim" because Tom surprised her with tickets to *Phantom of the Opera*.

There's Mariann, a graduate English student at the University of Maryland, the group's academic and token conservative. It was her idea to start a weekly sim newsletter. She's helped me out on more than one English paper ("Mariann! Emergency! How much do you know about the Allegory of the Cave in Plato's *Republic*?"), and amuses us all with her passionate support of the Republican Revolution.

There's West, an unabashed lady's man. He's probably the first person to receive an official warning from AOL for sexual harassment within the context of a role-playing game. He can drive us nuts, but Sim City wouldn't be the same without him. And there's Danica, my 3,000-miles-away twin. We started talking via e-mail when we realized we were taking the SAT the same day—and were amazed when we received identical scores. Our fast and furious conversation hasn't stopped since. Our similarities are uncanny: we've taken the same courses in school, been in many of the same plays, read the same books (no one else has ever understood my *Schrodinger's Cat* references!), agreed with the same philosophies, and laughed at the same jokes. We've co-written stories together, and our styles are indistinguishable. Two weeks ago, we finally met face to face when her dad came to D.C. for a conference and brought her along. We met up at Planet Hollywood in a mystery-novel-like scene: I stood outside in a black skirt with a braid over my shoulder, watching for a girl with short brown hair and a silver pentacle necklace. She slept over at my house, I played tour guide the next day, and we talked for 26 straight hours.

There's also Michael, Sue, Vic, Manda, Ruth, Jon, and a half dozen others who have become my extended family in the last year. Oh, I've heard the warnings about the Internet: you can't take anyone at face value; it's full of socially maladjusted kooks; the sense of community it creates is false; it'll ultimately drive people farther apart. I've read *Silicon Snake Oil* and listened on C-SPAN to Senator Exxon's diatribes about the evils of the information superhighway. But I've seen its virtues. I'm part of a generation growing up with this new communication medium, and I've found a place where I fit in among the thirty-seven million Internet users.

The America Online Thursday Sim Group is a community in every sense of the word. We met because of a common interest in creating a simulated world we can live in for a few hours a week, and have grown over the months to care about the people behind the characters. We remember birthdays, cheer each other up on bad days, celebrate accomplishments, and are there to just talk to, about everything from Jello to the afterlife. Like any family, we've had our spats (like the time when Mariann refused to run a story about Danica's character coming out of the closet, because it contradicted her idea of what values the sim should encourage), but we've been strong enough to overcome them. And if it weren't for our hidden corner, my 3,000-miles-away twin and I would never have met.

Essay No. 39

As a young boy, my father often took me to Wrigley Field. I was so intrigued by the sounds of the crowd mixed with the scent of hot dogs and peanuts in the air. The ivy clinging to the outfield walls contained memories of past seasons and the Cubs' losing tradition. As I analyze my attachment to this venerated shrine to baseball, I realize that my summer days working there helped me to mature, and taught me some sobering lessons. Other summer days relaxing in the bleachers suited my personality well.

In April of 1994, I began my summer job with the opening of the baseball season. During weekend games, I pushed a dessert cart from skybox to skybox, with the assignment to sell as many desserts as possible. It was fortunate that the success of the enterprise did not depend on my sales. Being somewhat shy with strangers, at first I had difficulty looking my customers in the eye. I stared down at the ground and mumbled the dessert choices. I am sure there was a universal feeling among the skybox guests that they were going deaf, as they always asked me to speak louder. The other employee assigned to the dessert cart always seemed to have more "tips" at the end of the day. That was when my sense of competition and pride took over. First I risked looking up; then I stopped mumbling; then I spoke louder; and to my surprise, I even started to have a confident personality with strangers. I was growing up, and I was proud of myself.

People all over the United States will remember the summer of 1994 as the summer of the baseball strike. I will remember it as the summer I got "laid off." I had always wanted to work at Wrigley Field, and was so proud of my new success. I was one happy fifteen-year old. By August, I had half my earnings saved for a new Kurzweil keyboard.

The tension was mounting as the playoffs and World Series approached. Another tension was also accelerating between the owners and the players, but I did not take it seriously. Then it happened. Suddenly, the scent of hot dogs was gone, and there was no one to see the ivy in full bloom. The players and owners had forgotten the perfection and beauty of the game. It was shocking to realize that my heroes caused me to lose my job; the millions of dollars they were making were not enough. I could not believe that my dream of a new keyboard was gone. This suddenly seemed insignificant when Javier, one of my co-workers, expressed his anxiety about feeding his family of five. I wondered how many other families would seriously suffer financially when their paychecks stopped arriving. The word "strike" in baseball now had a sobering new meaning.

My days as a fan in the bleachers reflect a completely different part of me. During my high school years, it has become a summertime hobby to attend as many games as possible. My reason for attending is never just to watch the game, for I find Wrigley Field to be a great place for reflection. I always sit in the bleachers, where the fans share my enthusiasm for the experience. Our emotions rise and fall together during the course of the game. On a perfect day, I sit shirtless in the warm sun, observing, reflecting and treasuring. My view is of home plate and the elegant architecture of downtown Chicago out of the corner of my eye. Being an optimist, I continue to have hope that one day the Cubs will win the World Series for the first time since 1908. But even if they never do, I will always feel part of a larger tradition and a coming of age.

Essay No. 40

Me? An athlete? No, you must be thinking of my brother. Well, maybe not. Yes, I am a proud, diligent member of Ramapo's winter track team. I drag myself to practice five or six days a week to run and run until my legs burn so much that they feel like they're about to explode. And I can't neglect to mention my ankles right after practice when I can hardly walk, my pounding head, and my so-smelly-don't-even-go-near-them running sneakers.

Now this may appear terrible, and you're probably wondering why I didn't quit months ago. The thing is, I'm not exactly sure either. When I'm sprinting the track or the circle in front of the school and I'm all sweaty and I keep stepping in puddles or sliding on ice, I often ask myself, "Why am I here? What am I doing?" I never come up with an answer, but I keep on running. If someone were to have predicted my future five years ago and told me that I'd be braving the tortures of Track in high school, I would have said, "Yeah, right. I don't think so." This is because I don't have a history of being the most athletically-inclined person. The only sports team that I played on was T-Ball, but I never really loved it, so I didn't go out for the team in third grade.

But now that I'm a runner I usually enjoy it, and I think that I have found my sport. It has taught me how to be a team player, how to focus on goals I set for myself, and how to push myself to the limit when I'm exhausted and discouraged. I'm proud of myself for attending practice every day, working as hard as I am able, and never giving up on the sport. Believe me, it would be very easy for me to quit, considering that I've never actually won a race. I have come in second, but it's not the same.

I had been feeling a little frustrated because of the lack of medals on my bare trophy wall. So I decided to talk to my coach about it. Being the emotional sap that I am, I started crying before I could even say what I had planned. He told me that when he was in high school, medals weren't exactly showered upon him either. In fact, he didn't win any. But during the summer before his senior year, he trained the hardest he ever had and when he stepped onto the track for his first meet, he won. He kept on winning until the quarterfinals of the 1988 Olympics, which I think is an amazing feat. He also competed against the rough and tough American Gladiators, which is also pretty impressive. He told me that I shouldn't give up because I had improved since the beginning of the season and I had potential. Thank God.

And now that the season is over, I have a better idea why I force myself to go to practice, even on weekends. I have this dream that maybe I will turn out like my coach—I definitely won't compete in the Olympics, but one day I'm going to win. I'm going to be first. And when I look at my now-empty trophy wall, I'm going to smile.

Essay No. 41

For my thirteenth birthday I received three juggling cubes. Made of soft patchy cloth and filled with a grainy substance, they were perfectly engineered for quick, slightly inaccurate catches. After fingering them for a few minutes, I decided that, despite my lack of coordination, I would learn to juggle. "It's a process," I thought, "and I am a savant of logic; I can compensate for my physical inadequacies with my logical thought." To celebrate my decision, I tossed one of the balls up with extreme gusto and promptly missed it with equally unmitigated exuberance.

I leafed through the book until I had a sufficient grasp of the principles of juggling. Feeling confident, I picked up the three balls and attempted to apply my knowledge. After several weeks of practice and hours of intensive analysis, I pinpointed my difficulty: the tendency of the balls to rush abruptly to the ground. I needed something slower. "Scarves," I thought, but subsequent near-catches with a broken lamp proved that a slower object wasn't the answer. In desperation, I dispensed with strategy, and instead began to throw the balls methodically. For the next week, I integrated juggling into my lifestyle. I would wake up, juggle drowsily, shower, dry off while juggling recklessly, juggle while lying in bed, and dream about juggling. My persistence became an obsession; balls danced about my head, cascades soared majestically over head, and swift pins flipped and spun in the corner of my eye.

The aforementioned is the story of how my interest in juggling began. After weeks of intensive practice, I mastered first the rudiments and then the intricacies of juggling. When I could finally execute complicated trick sequences, it was official: juggling was a hobby.

I enjoyed the change of pace, physical instead of intellectual, and the sense of power one feels when gravity is defied. The whizzing, spinning balls become an other-worldly creation; they move and dance in new and exciting ways. Once a dance has been mastered, I move on to another one. Whizz! Spin! I am the creator and the esthete, making and enjoying. Respin and back! The ball explores new territory. The once impossible is simple. Reverse and under! A balls goes through, and is replaced by a bowling pin. Smack! Reality hits suddenly and painfully.

Essay No. 42

[This essay responded to a question that asked the applicant to include a photograph of personal significance and explain that significance.]

"Shhuuut uuup!" yells my mother in French from the kitchen. The next moment, my brother is charging at me, eyes ablaze. My instinct is to run, but my escape route is blocked by my sister, who is waiting for me at the end of the hall with a sadistic look on her face. I am trapped. "I surrender!" I cry out. Flanking me like a military escort, brother and sister march me back to my room, where I am left alone—alone with my violin.

Please don't be alarmed. My family is not crazy, nor for that matter am I. The cause of all these extravagant goings-on in our home is the fiddle—more precisely, my slightly eccentric way of practicing it.

I have been playing the violin for twelve years, and for twelve years my family has had to hear me practice thousands of hours. It is quite reasonable to suppose that, after such constant and endless repetition of much the same notes, they might get a bit sensitive to those high-screeching and low-pounding sounds, resonating inside their ears and rattling their nervous systems. But it's not only the sounds that grate on them. Through the years, I have grown accustomed to walking around when I practice. The pieces I play excite in me such feeling, such passion, that I find it hard to stay in one place. My violin practice is, well, peripatetic.

A typical practice session goes something like this: after ambling around my room twenty-five or thirty times, I feel a need to venture outside its walls. So I swing into the hall. At once, my whole body is invaded by a feeling of great exhilaration. Gracefully, I lift the violin to my chin and flourish the bow high in the air. At this moment, I feel myself the equal of Heifetz or Perlman. Then, out of the instrument comes what is possibly the most aggravating sound known to man. In a flash, I am yanked back to reality and my family's nerve endings are set all aquiver.

To fully appreciate the effect of my playing on the others, you have to know that in our house all the main rooms open into the hallway that I have temporarily made my concert hall. Whatever sound is produced in this passage is heard throughout the house, its volume not just undiminished but actually increased, thanks to the hall's acoustics.

The notes I have scratched out are still hovering in the air when, from the kitchen, my mom peremptorily orders me to stop. Lost in the pleasure of playing, I pretend not to hear her. She then screams, which is a cue for my kid brother and sister to mount another of their sound-police assaults. I invariably end up being pushed back to where I started from. But I am never able to stay put, and before long I am launched on my customary circuit once again.

My violinistic vagabondage has so far proven to be incurable, but an incident a few years ago had a powerful tempering effect on it. I was then (and still am) a novice in the art of living with others harmoniously. I had started to practice, and in due course I had wandered to where my brother was doing his homework. He seemed to be in a state of intense concentration. I said to myself, "He needs to get away from his work for a bit," and so I began to crank out my latest piece. Strange to say, he failed to respond to the intricate meaning of the composition; nor did he seem to appreciate the fact that he was the first one for whom I had ever condescended to play the piece. Already in a bad mood, he didn't bother to ask me to stop playing. Instead, he jumped up from his chair and chased me furiously toward my room. As I prepared in my flight to make a sharp Road Runner turn, I slipped, and a moment later, with a sharp report, my bow snapped in two against the wall. For several seconds I stood staring at the broken halves, in shock. Even my brother let out a gasp. Then I started to panic. What was I going to tell my parents?

Hoping for leniency, I offered up a full confession to them. As punishment, I was made to pay for the broken bow. From that day to this, I have continued to annoy my family with my peripatetic practicing, but if anyone so much as raises his or her voice in complaint, into my room I promptly go.

For my application, the reason why I've chosen a photo of my violin and me cooped up in my closet is that in my family's eyes the closet is the ideal spot for me to practice. As a final note, and to erase any misconceptions I may have created by what I've said up to now, I ought to state that though I've sometimes used my violin as an instrument of annoyance and retaliation (and I modestly claim to have been quite successful in this department), I most of all use it to express my deepest feelings, whether I'm playing classical music, jazz, even rock'n roll. It is the voice of my truest self.

Essay No. 43

It was early May and the cherry blossoms were in full bloom as the sun shimmered between the passing clouds. Except for a mandatory essay assignment about one of the sights, it was a perfect day for a visit to the nation's capital. What I had not anticipated was a sleek, black memorial that angled out from the side of a hill. Gazing at the stark granite and the infinite list of names, I could not imagine choosing another sight to write about. So much emotion existed there. I simply had to transcribe those intangible feelings onto paper.

I wasn't very surprised to be included as one of the finalists in the "Best D.C. Essay Contest." I was, however, shocked to win first place in the eighth-grade division. The essay was then passed along to the President of the local VFW post, which was sponsoring a Memorial Day essay contest. Here, too, I won in the eighth-grade division. The awards were purely worldly items: a year's supply of Coca-Cola, a $25 check, and the chance to ride on a float in the City of Greensburg parade.

At the end of the parade, a ceremony followed. I stood up, walked over to the podium, and began:

"A young child rubs off the name of a grandfather seen only in photographs . . ."

I looked up and saw all the eyes on me. The nervous feelings that traveled with me from my seat to the podium were now long gone. The words I had written flowed easily from my mouth. I wanted everyone, even those who had never seen the Memorial, to feel the same sentiments that I had felt. I don't remember people clapping after I finished reading my essay.

Pearls of Wisdom about Applying for College Admission . . .

Realize that there are lots of options in higher education. Don't put all your eggs in one basket. You will have at least two or three good choices if you applied to a range of schools. Most students who do not get into Yale will get into other fine schools that offer equally extraordinary opportunities. Realize that there are many viable and wonderful possible outcomes.

At the outset of this process, step back and take a deep breath. Don't panic. Start early. Begin to conceive your college plans in your junior year. Look at the essay questions for the schools you are applying to as soon as you can. Spend thoughtful time approaching the process so that when you do complete your essay you feel good about it. Notify school officials early if you plan to apply. If you apply with a prepared, calm approach within a reasonable amount of time, then your outcome will be better than if you do a rush job.

Most of all, be yourself. Don't try to package yourself the way somebody else thinks you should. Starting now, think about your hopes and dreams and about who you are. Hopefully, all of this will come through in the way you express yourself to us so that we can determine if you are a good "fit" for Yale.

Have You Written A Great College Admission Essay?

Would you like to see it published in the next edition of *Best College Admission Essays*?

If so, submit your essay to the address below. Please include your mailing address and evidence of admission (such as a copy of a letter of acceptance). You will be contacted by mail only if the authors wish to include your essay in the book's next edition.

Send your college admission essay to:

Best College Admission Essays
c/o Thomson Peterson's
Princeton Pike Corporate Center
2000 Lenox Drive
Lawrenceville, NJ 08648

NOTES

NOTES

NOTES

NOTES